AF716581

Control Premiums: Application & Analysis

A BVR Special Report

BVR
What It's Worth
Business Valuation Resources, LLC
1000 SW Broadway, Suite 1200
Portland, OR 97205
(503) 291-7963 Fax • (503) 291-7955 • www.BVResources.com

BVR

What It's Worth

Copyright © 2010 by Business Valuation Resources, L.L.C. (BVR). All rights reserved.

Printed in the United States of America.

No part of this publication may be reproduced, stored in a retrieval system or transmitted in any form or by any means, electronic, mechanical, photocopying, recording, scanning or otherwise, except as permitted under Sections 107 or 108 of the 1976 United States Copyright Act, without either the prior written permission of the Publisher or authorization through payment of the appropriate per copy fee to the Publisher. Requests for permission should be addressed to the Permissions Department, Business Valuation Resources, LLC, 1000 SW Broadway St., Suite 1200, Portland, OR, 97205, (503) 291-7963, fax (503) 291-7955.

Information contained in this book has been obtained by Business Valuation Resources from sources believed to be reliable. However, neither Business Valuation Resources nor its authors guarantee the accuracy or completeness of any information published herein and neither Business Valuation Resources nor its authors shall be responsible for any errors, omissions, or damages arising out of use of this information. This work is published with the understanding that Business Valuation Resources and its authors are supplying information but are not attempting to render business valuation or other professional services. If such services are required, the assistance of an appropriate professional should be sought.

Managing Editor: Colin Murcray
Publisher: Doug Twitchell

Chair and CEO: David Foster
President: Lucretia Lyons
Sales: Linda Mendenhall
Customer Service Manager: Stephanie Crader

ISBN: 978-1-935081-39-5

Table of Contents

Control Premiums: Application and Analysis. 1
By: Brad Pursel, CPA/ABV, CFA, ASA

Misuse of Control Premiums in Delaware Appraisals 13
by Gilbert E. Matthews, CFA

Implied Minority Discount in Statutory Fair Value: The Doctrine that Just Won't Die 28

General Analysis from the Mergerstat®/BVR Control Premium Study™ 31

Teleconference Transcript & Presentation Slides
Control Premiums: Applications & Analysis 33
April 29, 2010
Brad Pursel, CPA/ABV, CFA, ASA
Mark J. Edwards, CPA/ABV, CFA
Andrew S. Fargason, CFA

Court Case Abstracts

ASARCO v. Americas Mining Corp. 83
Stuart Agranoff, et al. v. Edward M. Miller, et al. 87
Kathryn Casey v. Amboy Bancorporation 88
Cede & Co. v. JRC Acquisition Corp., et al. 91
Eateries, Inc. v. J.R. Simplot Co. 93
Framatome Connectors USA, Inc. and Subsidiaries, et al. v. CIR 94
Gagliano v. Brennan (I) 96
Gotham Partners, L.P. v. Hallwood Realty Partners, L.P., et al. 97
Highfields Capital, Ltd. v. AXA Financial, Inc.. 99
Lane v. Cancer Treatment Centers of America, Inc. 103
Estate of Mary D. Maggos v. CIR. 105
Estate of Magnin v. Commissioner (II). 108
Northwest Investment Corp. v. Wallace 109
Estate of Simplot v. Commissioner (II) 111
Slattery v. U.S.. 115
In re Toys "R" Us, Inc., Shareholder Litigation 117

Disclaimer for Telephone Conference Transcript: Business Valuation Resources, LLC, believes this transcript to be an accurate representation of the telephone conference. This is not, however, a verbatim transcript of the conference recording as minor edits have been made to improve readability.

BVR

What It's Worth

Control Premiums: Application and Analysis

By: Brad Pursel, CPA/ABV, CFA, ASA
bpursel@bswllc.com

Most valuation specialists would likely agree that the selection of a control premium is an exercise that requires significant "appraiser's judgment." This would be true whether valuing a controlling interest or calculating the inverse of a control premium to value a noncontrolling interest. Besides the magnitude of a control premium, the appropriateness of even including a control premium (or discount for lack of control) is not beyond debate in a particular valuation. For instance, the application of a control premium introduces an assumption that may be faulty in many instances: since many public companies have been acquired at a premium to their then traded-value, there exists a willing buyer for *every* public company who would be willing to pay a premium to the publicly-traded value.[1]

This paper provides an overview of control premiums, data sources, typical analytical framework for control premiums, and an analysis of the factors that are commonly believed to influence the magnitude of control premiums.

Overview of Control Premiums

Control premium is defined as follows: "an amount or a percentage by which the pro rata value of a controlling interest exceeds the pro rata value of a noncontrolling interest in a business enterprise to reflect the power of control."[2] *Control* is defined as "the power to direct the management, dominate the decision making process and set the policies of a business enterprise."[3] Control and the impact of control (or lack thereof) are an important consideration in any valuation. According to the Uniform Standards of Professional Appraisal Practice ("USPAP") (Standards Rule 9-2dii), an appraiser *must* "ascertain the extent to which the interests contain elements of ownership control."

There are two primary uses of control premium data: 1) adjusting value indications on a noncontrolling interest basis (such as that derived using the guideline public company method) *upwards* to be comparable to a controlling interest basis; and 2) after calculating the inverse of the control premium to derive an implied discount for lack of control, adjusting value indications on a controlling interest basis (such as that derived using the mergers and acquisitions method) *downwards* to be comparable to a noncontrolling interest basis.[4] In addition to the above, financial advisory firms often utilize control premium data in advising board of directors and drafting fairness opinions by assessing the reasonableness of an offer to acquire a publicly-traded company via an assessment of the implied control premium relative to selected benchmark transactions.[5]

In selecting control premiums, much focus is typically placed on finding transaction data that is deemed relevant to a subject company valuation based upon certain criteria, which may include the similarity of the industry underlying the transaction data to the subject company, the proximity of the transaction date to the valuation date, and the type of buyer (i.e., strategic or financial buyer), among other factors. However, historically there has been little attention as to whether the price paid to obtain control and, therefore, control premium, are related to factors *other than* those typically considered. After all, control premiums are perhaps more accurately described as *acquisition* premiums that include

1 Gilbert E. Matthews, "Misuse of Control Premiums in Delaware Appraisals", *Business Valuation Review*, Summer 2008. Also, see Shannon P. Pratt, *Business Valuation Discounts and Premiums*, Chapter 2 (2009). Lengthy discussion of this topic is included in "The Value of Control: Implications for Control Premia, Minority Discounts and Voting Share Differentials", white paper, Aswath Damodaran, (June 2005).

2 Per International Glossary of Business Valuation Terms.

3 Ibid.

4 Formulae to calculate inverse of control premium include: 1-(1/(1+control premium) and control premium/(1+control premium).

5 Philip J. Clements and Philip W. Wisler, *The Standard & Poor's Guide to Fairness Opinions: A User's Guide for Fiduciaries* (2005).

a multitude of factors influencing the ultimate price and, therefore, premium paid to acquire a company.[6] Negotiation prowess (or lack thereof) and potential "winner's curse" are certainly elements to consider, particularly considering the often cited mixed track record for most acquisitions. In terms of analyzing and selecting control premiums to use in a valuation, the potential exists that control premiums are driven by factors that are largely ignored by valuation specialists.

Sources of Control Premium Data

Mergerstat Review® annually examines transactions involving companies whose stocks are publicly traded. The publication then calculates the premium paid by the acquiring company over the acquired company's stock price prior to the announced offer. Various iterations of the control premium are provided varying by time period prior to offer date. In addition, Mergerstat also calculates and reports on a measure called the Mergerstat® Unaffected Control Premium, which purports to be based upon a stock price unaffected by the rumors that may have preceded any public disclosure regarding the acquisition. The analysis in this article focuses on this unaffected control premium as this appears to be the premium used by most valuation specialists who consult this data source. *Mergerstat®/BVR Control Premium Study*™ is an online tool offering great flexibility to any control premium search. In addition, transaction databases, including *Capital IQ* and *FactSet*, have search and reporting criteria that enable an analyst to perform a control premium search. The availability of online databases reporting control premium data significantly increases the ease at which an analyst can access and analyze numerous variables deemed relevant to a control premium assessment. For this article, data available from the *Mergerstat®/BVR Control Premium Study*™ was utilized.[7]

6 *Control Premia Teleconference Transcript*, August 24, 2006, Aswath Damodaran, Kenneth Woo, Anna Berhelius. Damodaran suggests, in addition to control, factors to consider include: information leakage, which impacts measurement of "true" acquisition premium; motives of buyers, which may include synergies; undervalued stock; and management hubris or "stupid premium." Lastly, Damodaran certain types of firms are more likely to become acquisition targets than other firms.

7 The analysis presented includes sorts of transaction data by percentage of stock acquired, which generally varied from levels of 80% to 100%, depending upon the relationship being measured. For instance, when sorting transaction data in terms of debt to total capital, only transactions where 100% of stock acquired were included in the analysis. Negative control premiums were included in the data analyzed unless noted otherwise.

Control Premiums in Financial Reporting

Potentially applicable in a valuation engagement for any purpose, control premiums have most recently received significant attention in the context of financial reporting. FAS 142 explicitly addressed the potential applicability of control premiums in goodwill impairment testing. Per paragraph 23 as amended by FAS 157: "Quoted market prices in active markets are the best evidence of fair value and shall be used as the basis for the measurement, if available. However, the market price of an individual equity security (and thus the market capitalization of a reporting unit with publicly traded equity securities) may not be representative of the fair value of the reporting unit as a whole. *Substantial value may arise from the ability to take advantage of synergies and other benefits that flow from control over another entity* (emphasis added). Consequently, measuring the fair value of a collection of assets and liabilities that operate together in a controlled entity is different from measuring the fair value of that entity's individual equity securities. An acquiring entity often is willing to pay more for equity securities that give it a controlling interest than an investor would pay for a number of equity securities representing less than a controlling interest. That control premium may cause the fair value of a reporting unit to exceed its market capitalization."

Control premiums took on greater importance in late 2008 as the significant downturn in equity markets led to perhaps unprecedented levels of goodwill impairments. During impairment testing under FAS 142, one of the more common topics of debate concerned the magnitude of control premiums that were appropriate. Management at public companies, dismayed at the seemingly irrational pricing of their stock following a sudden and significant decline in value, frequently argued that the stock prices did not reflect intrinsic value. Therefore, management argued that a larger than "average" control premium would be necessary to derive an appropriate value for the company.[8] Otherwise, the argument was made that the company's board of directors would never sell the company at the price indicated.

8 *BV Wire #77-1*, "SEC resists 'bright line rule' on control premiums – but still wants to see adequate support from appraisers. Referring to speech by Evan Sussholtz of the SEC, for use of a control premium falling outside of range of prior transactions, SEC would "expect to see more analysis of cash flows, benefits of control, market participant analysis."

As a result of the frequency of the above debate, The Appraisal Foundation decided to form a Working Group in 2009 to study control premiums in hopes of developing "best practice" guidance related to the application of control premiums in valuation engagements for financial reporting purposes. In addition, the AICPA has formed a task force on impairment testing who may, among other topics, address the application of control premiums in a forthcoming practice aid.

Framework for Control Premium Analysis

As previously mentioned, valuation specialists conducting a control premium analysis typically focus on transactions that are deemed appropriate based upon certain criteria, which may include the similarity of the target's industry to the subject company, the proximity of the transaction date to the valuation date, and the buyer type (i.e., strategic or financial buyer), among others.[9] By buyer type, a distinction is attempted to be made as to whether the premium paid truly relates to control or, in fact, is more of a synergistic premium that is not related solely to obtaining control. However, historically there has been little attention as to whether the price paid to obtain control and, therefore, control premium, are related to factors not typically being captured by the above criteria or search screens. In addition, there are other factors used by some valuation specialists to adjust control premiums, including differences between the capital structure among the target companies and the subject company. Although such an adjustment has theoretical appeal, quantitative support for such an adjustment has not been provided.

Methods to Apply a Control Premium

Below is a description of the three methods used to convert a value indication on a noncontrolling basis to a controlling interest basis through the application of a control premium.

9 Buyer attitude have been theorized by some authors, including Damodaran, as another factor to consider in control premiums. However, data limitations may limit usefulness of this transaction screen criteria. For instance, out of the 7,007 transactions reviewed in the *Mergerstat®/BVR Control Premium Database*, only 42 were described as being "hostile in nature.

1. Unadjusted Equity Premium – calculated or selected equity control premium (percentage) is applied to equity of subject company

2. Invested Capital or Enterprise Value Premium – calculated or selected control premium (in dollar terms) is divided by invested capital (i.e., entity value) to estimate the control premium (in percentage terms) relative to invested capital.

3. Adjusted Equity Premium – calculated or selected equity control premium (percentage) is adjusted for differences between the capital structure of the target company and the subject company by scaling the control premium higher (lower) if the target company's equity/total capital level is higher (lower) than the subject company. This method is related to Method 2 discussed above and, assuming consistent data inputs, would result in the same value if used to value the subject company.

The implication from the use of Methods 2 and 3 are that a control premium is entirely or partially tied to the overall value of the target company rather than the equity of the target company. The basis for such an argument would be that a key driver of the magnitude of a control premium is the level of synergies that a buyer would be expected to derive from the acquisition and such synergies are more appropriately measured relative to the value of the overall business, regardless of its capital structure. The distinction between the above methods is important when applying a control premium to a company with a different capital structure than the target companies underlying the control premium data analyzed. For Methods 2 and 3 to be appropriate, an analysis of control premium data would need to show that the magnitude of equity control premiums (in percentage terms would increase (decrease) as the level of debt in the target's capital structure increased (decreased). For example, assume that a company with a pre-acquisition invested capital value of $100 million was acquired for $120 million and, therefore, a $20 million premium was paid. Below is an illustration of the variability in the implied equity control premium (in percentage terms) based upon different capital structure assumptions for the target company.

Debt/Capital	Equity Control Premium	Invested Capital Control Premium
0.0%	20.0%	20.0%
5.0%	26.3%	20.0%
10.0%	33.3%	20.0%
15.0%	41.2%	20.0%
20.0%	50.0%	20.0%
25.0%	60.0%	20.0%
30.0%	71.4%	20.0%
35.0%	84.6%	20.0%
40.0%	100.0%	20.0%
45.0%	118.2%	20.0%
50.0%	140.0%	20.0%

Based upon the preceding discussion, there are two clear issues to address: First, are control premiums from strategic buyers higher than those paid by financial buyers? Second, are control premiums more related to equity values or measures related to the overall value of a business, such as invested capital? In addition, this article will also consider other variables, including recent academic research applicable to control premium analysis.

Impact of Buyer Type on Control Premiums

The common perception is that strategic buyers (vertical, horizontal, etc.) are perceived to benefit from synergies, which either result in higher combined revenues and/or lower costs, which increase the value of the acquired entity over the value to a financial buyer. Therefore, financial buyers are presumed to be more reflective of "pure" perquisites of control. (Note: due to the presence of financial buyers, such as private equity firms, with portfolio companies that may derive synergies from an acquisition, the labeling of a buyer as either "strategic" or "financial" can require additional analysis beyond simply looking at the name of the buyer). Again, as stated in FAS 142, "Substantial value may arise from the ability to take advantage of synergies and other benefits that flow from control over another entity." Such a distinction is potentially important if, in applying a control premium to a particular subject company, the belief is that the likely buyer would be a financial buyer or perhaps if the perception is that there are fewer synergistic benefits to be generated through an acquisition of the subject company. In addition, when the inverse of the control premium is used to estimate a minority interest discount, then the inclusion of an inflated control premium due to perceived synergies would be inappropriate as these reflect value attributed to something other than sole control of the business. As a result, for a valuation of a company in a particular industry, the pool of transactions used in a control premium analysis may vary depending upon assumptions regarding the identity of the willing buyer or market participants and whether the valuation is of a controlling interest or the control premium data will be used to estimate a discount for lack of control.

Overall, the implication from the above discussion is that control premiums derived from transactions with strategic buyers should be higher than those derived from transactions with financial buyers. On the following page is a summary of analysis related to control premium by buyer type.[10]

As shown, the frequency of strategic and financial buyers increases as the size of the control premium decreases, while the frequency of horizontal control premiums decreases as the size of the control premium decreases. Overall, the frequency of buyer types that is expected to include more synergistic benefits (Strategic/Vertical/Horizontal) is fairly consistent for control premiums above 20% and decreases slightly for control premiums below 20%.

Also on the following page is a summary of average control premiums by buyer type for a sample of SIC Codes for which a significant number of transactions existed.

The results from this analysis of control premiums by buyer type is mixed. There does not appear to be a consistent pattern indicating that the control premiums paid by financial buyers are lower than those paid by non-financial buyers. As such, it is possible the size of a control premium is more driven by factors other than buyer type. Possible explanations include that the sample of transactions with financial versus non-financial buyers is too heterogeneous, including differences in composition in terms of industry, country, capital structure, target stock exchange, acquisition year, etc. The number of transactions in the source database involving financial/conglomerate buyers is also significantly less than that involving other buyer types. It is possible that certain buyers labeled as

10 Buyer types are defined by Mergerstat.

All Transactions (Positive Control Premiums Only)								
		Buyer Type						
Mergerstat Control Premium	Transaction Count	Strategic	Vertical	Horizontal	Financial	Conglomerate	Strategic / Vertical / Horizontal	Financial / Conglomerate
>=100%	487	163	4	237	76	7	404	83
90% to 99%	109	39	4	55	11	0	98	11
80% to 89%	155	55	1	73	24	2	129	26
70% to 79%	200	76	2	89	31	2	167	33
60% to 69%	317	98	6	156	54	3	260	57
50% to 59%	421	149	4	198	69	1	351	70
40% to 49%	503	196	7	211	85	4	414	89
30% to 39%	780	328	13	320	113	6	661	119
20% to 29%	987	416	10	383	166	12	809	178
10% to 19%	1,021	447	11	353	203	7	811	210
1% to 9%	834	368	5	263	192	6	636	198
Total	5,814	2,335	67	2,338	1,024	50	4,740	1,074
Percentage of Total								
>=100%	100.0%	33.5%	0.8%	48.7%	15.6%	1.4%	83.0%	17.0%
90% to 99%	100.0%	35.8%	3.7%	50.5%	10.1%	0.0%	89.9%	10.1%
80% to 89%	100.0%	35.5%	0.6%	47.1%	15.5%	1.3%	83.2%	16.8%
70% to 79%	100.0%	38.0%	1.0%	44.5%	15.5%	1.0%	83.5%	16.5%
60% to 69%	100.0%	30.9%	1.9%	49.2%	17.0%	0.9%	82.0%	18.0%
50% to 59%	100.0%	35.4%	1.0%	47.0%	16.4%	0.2%	83.4%	16.6%
40% to 49%	100.0%	39.0%	1.4%	41.9%	16.9%	0.8%	82.3%	17.7%
30% to 39%	100.0%	42.1%	1.7%	41.0%	14.5%	0.8%	84.7%	15.3%
20% to 29%	100.0%	42.1%	1.0%	38.8%	16.8%	1.2%	82.0%	18.0%
10% to 19%	100.0%	43.8%	1.1%	34.6%	19.9%	0.7%	79.4%	20.6%
1% to 9%	100.0%	44.1%	0.6%	31.5%	23.0%	0.7%	76.3%	23.7%
Total	100.0%	40.2%	1.2%	40.2%	17.6%	0.9%	81.5%	18.5%

Average Mergerstat Control Premium								
			Buyer Type					
SIC Code	Description	Count	Strategic	Vertical	Horizontal	Strategic/ Vertical/ Horizontal	Financial/ Conglomerate	All
1311	Crude Petroleum and Natural Gas	263	18.9%		30.2%	25.4%	25.5%	25.4%
2834	Pharmaceutical Preparations	130	65.1%	82.9%	53.3%	60.1%	101.1%	61.7%
3577	Computer Peripheral Equipment, NEC	35	36.7%		21.5%	25.8%	20.9%	25.4%
3823	Industrial Instruments for Measurement, Display, and Control	31	26.0%		34.9%	30.6%	47.3%	32.8%
3841	Surgical and Medical Instruments and Apparatus	60	46.1%		75.8%	54.4%	98.9%	58.8%
7371	Computer Programming Services	77	40.4%	45.3%	26.1%	32.3%	129.6%	41.2%
7372	Prepackaged Software	455	40.9%	69.3%	40.2%	40.8%	31.1%	39.6%
7373	Computer Integrated Systems Design	103	38.9%	41.2%	33.1%	35.3%	34.4%	35.2%
7374	Computer Processing and Data Preparation and Processing	37	25.9%		17.8%	20.2%	19.4%	20.0%
7375	Information Retrieval Services	45	32.4%	-33.7%	19.2%	28.0%	9.8%	24.3%
7379	Computer Related Services, NEC	57	35.0%		37.5%	36.4%	27.4%	35.4%

financial (strategic) buyers in fact have characteristics that would enable those buyers to generate higher (lower) synergies than otherwise expected. Lastly, it is possible the impact of buyer type on control premiums must be measured using statistical techniques not utilized in this article.

Equity vs. Invested Capital Control Premium

Despite the seemingly sound basis to consider the dollar control premium relative to measures of business value (such as invested capital or business enterprise value) to generate a percentage control premium, there should be a consideration as to whether the control premium data actually supports such a calculation. In order to compare the control premiums calculated under each method (specifically, Method 1 and Method 3 described previously), the coefficient of variation statistic is utilized. *Coefficient of variation*, which is measured by dividing standard deviation by mean, is a relative measure of variability and, therefore, is useful for comparing the variability of variables that have different standard deviations and different means. A lower coefficient of variation ("CoV") can be interpreted to mean that the variable under consideration has lower variability or greater consistency than another variable. Therefore, I calculated the coefficient of variation of control premiums based upon equity and invested capital in order to determine which variable was more consistent and, therefore, potentially a more relevant basis for calculating control premiums from transaction data and applying such control premiums to other companies.

Below is a summary of the analysis performed. Initially, I considered the coefficient of variation by buyer type by year and then by SIC Code.

As shown, the coefficient of variation for the equity control premium was typically lower than the coefficient of variation for the invested capital control premium. The tables on the following page show coefficient of variations for the equity and invested capital control premiums after segregating the target companies into more homogeneous capital structure.[11]

11 Transactions grouped into by ranges of debt capital levels. For instance,"0.0%" captures target companies with less than 1.0% debt/capital; "10.0%" debt/capital captures target companies with debt levels from 1.0% to 9.99%; "20.0%" captures target companies with debt levels from 10.1% to 19.99%, and so on.

Coefficient of Variation			
All Transactions			
Year	Equity Control Premium	Invested Capital Control Premium	Equity Lower?
All	1.48	1.56	Yes
2009	1.07	1.04	No
2008	1.49	1.31	No
2007	1.13	1.20	Yes
2006	1.14	1.21	Yes
2005	1.19	1.35	Yes
2004	1.26	1.35	Yes
2003	1.00	1.16	Yes
2002	1.75	1.56	No
2001	1.88	2.12	Yes
2000	1.57	1.83	Yes

Coefficient of Variation			
Strategic/Vertical/Horizontal Buyers			
Year	Equity Control Premium	Invested Capital Control Premium	Equity Lower?
All	1.48	1.55	Yes
2009	0.97	0.96	No
2008	1.57	1.37	No
2007	1.14	1.23	Yes
2006	1.12	1.19	Yes
2005	1.11	1.21	Yes
2004	1.26	1.35	Yes
2003	0.99	1.13	Yes
2002	1.78	1.59	No
2001	1.86	1.98	Yes
2000	1.64	1.89	Yes

Coefficient of Variation			
Strategic Buyers			
Year	Equity Control Premium	Invested Capital Control Premium	Equity Lower?
All	1.32	1.30	No
2009	0.97	0.96	No
2008	1.57	1.37	No
2007	1.14	1.23	Yes
2006	1.12	1.19	Yes
2005	1.11	1.20	Yes
2004	1.26	1.34	Yes
2003	0.99	1.13	Yes
2002	1.58	1.24	No

Coefficient of Variation			
SIC Code 3XXX			
Year	Equity Control Premium	Invested Capital Control Premium	Equity Lower?
All	1.28	1.34	Yes

Coefficient of Variation			
SIC Code 737X			
Year	Equity Control Premium	Invested Capital Control Premium	Equity Lower?
All	1.64	1.72	Yes

Coefficient of Variation			
SIC Code 2834-7			
Year	Equity Control Premium	Invested Capital Control Premium	Equity Lower?
All	1.27	1.26	No

All Industries - All Countries - All Buyers								
Debt / Capital	Count	Equity CP Average	IC CP Average	Equity CP Standard Deviation	IC CP Standard Deviation	Equity CP Coefficient of Variation	IC CP Coefficient of Variation	Equity CoV Lower?
0.0%	946	33.2%	33.1%	57.5%	57.0%	1.73	1.72	No
10.0%	891	30.6%	29.2%	43.2%	39.2%	1.41	1.34	No
20.0%	687	28.1%	24.0%	46.2%	31.1%	1.64	1.30	No
30.0%	523	31.9%	23.9%	39.6%	23.9%	1.24	1.00	No
40.0%	506	32.0%	20.9%	49.1%	20.5%	1.53	0.98	No
50.0%	393	33.3%	18.3%	44.6%	16.8%	1.34	0.92	No
60.0%	303	36.9%	16.7%	60.5%	16.7%	1.64	1.00	No
70.0%	213	42.7%	15.2%	50.2%	10.2%	1.18	0.67	No
80.0%	140	54.4%	13.7%	78.8%	14.9%	1.45	1.08	No
90.0%	108	56.6%	8.6%	73.3%	15.1%	1.29	1.77	Yes
100.0%	63	56.0%	2.9%	52.6%	4.5%	0.94	1.57	Yes

All Industries - U.S. Target Companies Only - All Buyers								
Debt / Capital	Count	Equity CP Average	IC CP Average	Equity CP Standard Deviation	IC CP Standard Deviation	Equity CP Coefficient of Variation	IC CP Coefficient of Variation	Equity CoV Lower?
0.0%	716	36.8%	36.7%	60.2%	59.7%	1.64	1.63	No
10.0%	562	33.0%	31.6%	41.3%	37.2%	1.25	1.18	No
20.0%	404	29.9%	25.5%	44.1%	30.4%	1.48	1.19	No
30.0%	309	34.5%	25.8%	41.3%	24.6%	1.20	0.95	No
40.0%	315	35.4%	23.1%	47.5%	20.1%	1.34	0.87	No
50.0%	247	32.4%	17.9%	42.5%	16.2%	1.31	0.90	No
60.0%	200	37.1%	16.7%	69.1%	16.6%	1.86	0.99	No
70.0%	115	39.5%	14.1%	44.2%	10.1%	1.12	0.71	No
80.0%	92	48.7%	12.4%	93.3%	14.4%	1.92	1.16	No
90.0%	65	63.2%	9.5%	83.4%	16.5%	1.32	1.73	Yes
100.0%	34	96.0%	4.6%	61.1%	5.1%	0.64	1.12	Yes

All Industries - All Countries - Strategic, Vertical, or Horizontal Buyers								
Debt / Capital	Count	Equity CP Average	IC CP Average	Equity CP Standard Deviation	IC CP Standard Deviation	Equity CP Coefficient of Variation	IC CP Coefficient of Variation	Equity CoV Lower?
0.0%	848	33.3%	33.2%	55.3%	55.0%	1.66	1.66	No
10.0%	770	30.3%	28.9%	44.1%	40.1%	1.46	1.39	No
20.0%	593	28.3%	24.1%	46.0%	31.3%	1.63	1.30	No
30.0%	441	33.2%	24.9%	41.9%	25.2%	1.26	1.01	No
40.0%	409	32.2%	21.0%	48.8%	21.0%	1.51	1.00	No
50.0%	313	33.9%	18.7%	45.1%	17.6%	1.33	0.95	No
60.0%	246	37.3%	16.9%	62.5%	17.5%	1.68	1.04	No
70.0%	173	42.9%	15.2%	51.4%	10.5%	1.20	0.69	No
80.0%	109	52.6%	13.1%	81.0%	15.6%	1.54	1.19	No
90.0%	87	59.5%	9.0%	67.2%	15.7%	1.13	1.75	Yes
100.0%	49	43.9%	2.1%	44.1%	3.1%	1.00	1.50	Yes

As shown on the previous page, when sorting target companies by debt to total capital levels, with the exception of some of the highest levels of debt to total capital, the coefficient of variation for the invested capital control premiums are consistently lower than the coefficient of variation for the equity control premiums, which implies that the invested capital control premiums exhibit less variability than the equity control premiums. The results from this analysis is consistent with the theory that control premiums are partially attributable and justified by buyers through the expected generation of synergies, which are logically more associated with the value of the overall business entity irrespective of capital structure. Below are potential implications from this data:

- Invested capital control premium should receive additional consideration in the analysis and selection of control premiums by valuation specialists and the assessment of control premiums by financial advisory firms and target company board of directors;

- High level of control premium variability at higher level of debt levels may reflect factors unrelated to synergies, such as potential bankruptcy risks, which may have been depressing the stock price of certain target companies; and

- Capital structure differences between target companies underlying control premium data and subject company under valuation should be considered before calculating implied discounts for lack of control.

Impact of Country and Stock Exchange on Control Premiums

Transaction and control premium databases often provide data for all geographic markets and stock exchanges. Financial theory indicates that the extent of market efficiency is not equal across geographic markets and stock exchanges. Under the guideline public company method, valuation specialists typically consider factors such as trading volume and float, removing companies where the trading volume or float is too low to reflect a reasonable indication of fair value for the overall company. However, in certain databases, trading volume and float statistics are either not reported for the publicly-traded stock of the seller companies or need to be accessed through additional searches. Without screening by geographic market and/or stock exchange, the assumption made by a valuation specialist is that the pre-transaction price of the seller companies has the same level of reliability or efficiency regardless of the target company's location, stock exchange listing, trading volume, float, etc.

I calculated average control premiums - in terms of both equity and invested capital - for certain target company countries in order to compare the relative magnitude of this statistic across countries. As shown on the following page, although there is significant variability among the countries, the average control premiums for the countries reporting large number of transactions (i.e., United States, Canada, England/United Kingdom, Australia) are generally within a tighter range.

I also calculated average control premiums by target exchange. Due to the significant number of transactions in the U.S. and Canada, I focused on the exchanges in these countries.

As shown on the followin page, there are significant differences in control premium by equity in comparing certain exchanges, which could partially be explained by differences in capital structure among target companies listed on each exchange. However, differences persist even controlling for capital structure by calculating invested capital control premiums. Therefore, control premium levels may reflect such diverse factors as listing criteria, industry composition, and factors effecting market efficiency, such as trading volume, acquisition dates, analyst coverage of stocks, etc. In addition, these factors should be considered before calculating implied discounts for lack of control as higher control premium levels for some companies may be indicative of factors reflecting a liquidity discount to the publicly-traded stock price. As a result, the valuation specialist should be wary of including such transactions in selecting control premiums or calculating an implied discount for lack of control which mixes characteristics of control with those of marketability.

Equity Control Premium by Target Country										
	All Buyers		Stategic / Vertical / Horizontal		Financial / Conglomerate		SIC Code 3XXX		SIC Code 737X	
Target Country	Count	Average	Count	Average	Count	Average	Count	Average	Count	Average
Australia	198	30.7%	175	30.6%	23	30.7%	13	32.1%	12	24.2%
Canada	693	32.3%	584	32.1%	109	33.5%	74	39.2%	79	47.0%
England	406	37.9%	301	38.8%	105	35.3%	71	40.3%	27	43.0%
Finland	14	13.3%	9	-9.5%	5	54.2%	4	28.3%	3	7.1%
France	52	19.6%	45	20.5%	7	13.8%	10	10.7%	14	13.4%
Hong Kong	15	12.0%	9	10.6%	6	14.1%	4	21.5%	1	-21.9%
Italy	20	32.5%	16	38.3%	4	9.3%	4	12.9%	0	n/a
Malaysia	14	14.4%	5	30.0%	9	5.7%	0	n/a	1	14.6%
Mexico	8	37.3%	7	43.1%	1	-2.8%	2	7.6%	0	n/a
New Zealand	11	44.9%	9	47.7%	2	32.4%	2	84.6%	0	n/a
Norway	49	27.5%	41	29.5%	8	17.0%	10	42.7%	9	22.1%
Singapore	31	19.8%	20	14.1%	11	30.3%	14	10.2%	2	19.4%
South Africa	33	24.1%	22	26.7%	11	18.8%	3	54.3%	3	76.9%
Spain	21	83.2%	15	109.0%	6	18.7%	1	73.3%	0	n/a
Sweden	79	35.4%	65	37.5%	14	25.4%	21	48.1%	15	30.9%
Taiwan	26	13.7%	23	12.7%	3	21.2%	10	4.9%	1	8.9%
United Kingdom	196	31.8%	128	30.7%	68	33.8%	26	45.0%	35	40.4%
United States	3,659	36.9%	3,202	36.7%	457	38.7%	689	40.4%	528	37.9%

Invested Capital Control Premium by Target Country										
	All Buyers		Stategic / Vertical /		Financial /		SIC Code 3XXX		SIC Code 737X	
Target Country	Count	Average	Count	Average	Count	Average	Count	Average	Count	Average
Australia	198	28.8%	175	29.5%	23	23.6%	13	23.6%	12	24.6%
Canada	693	27.3%	584	26.9%	109	29.1%	74	37.8%	79	51.0%
England	406	25.0%	301	26.3%	105	21.4%	71	25.5%	27	35.0%
Finland	14	0.3%	9	-7.4%	5	14.3%	4	18.7%	3	5.1%
France	52	9.4%	45	8.4%	7	16.0%	10	9.5%	14	-3.4%
Hong Kong	15	8.9%	9	5.6%	6	13.8%	4	14.7%	1	-21.9%
Italy	20	18.8%	16	21.7%	4	7.2%	4	10.0%	0	n/a
Malaysia	14	17.2%	5	40.0%	9	4.5%	0	n/a	1	75.9%
Mexico	8	30.6%	7	35.4%	1	-2.8%	2	5.0%	0	n/a
New Zealand	11	27.6%	9	27.4%	2	28.7%	2	40.5%	0	n/a
Norway	49	6.8%	41	6.1%	8	10.4%	10	31.0%	9	18.8%
Singapore	31	70.9%	20	11.7%	11	178.6%	14	9.2%	2	18.5%
South Africa	33	10.1%	22	7.0%	11	16.4%	3	50.5%	3	38.5%
Spain	21	23.1%	15	27.5%	6	12.0%	1	17.8%	0	n/a
Sweden	79	23.9%	65	29.2%	14	-0.5%	21	36.2%	15	43.5%
Taiwan	26	5.5%	23	3.6%	3	20.4%	10	-0.9%	1	8.2%
United Kingdom	196	24.1%	128	24.7%	68	23.0%	26	36.5%	35	28.7%
United States	3,659	28.4%	3,202	28.8%	457	25.6%	689	32.2%	528	34.0%

Equity Control Premium		
U.S. and Canadian Exchanges		
Exchange	Count	Average
NYSE	873	30.6%
Nasdaq	2,214	37.7%
Amex	203	31.1%
Over-the-Counter	417	47.6%
Toronto	467	32.2%
Canadian Venture	147	61.1%

Invested Capital Control Premium		
U.S. and Canadian Exchanges		
Exchange	Count	Average
NYSE	850	21.1%
Nasdaq	2,150	31.0%
Amex	194	22.2%
Over-the-Counter	410	35.6%
Toronto	439	23.1%
Canadian Venture	134	50.2%

Other Factors Impacting Control Premiums

In assessing control premiums, it is important to consider the environment in which offers are made and assessed for public companies. A company's board of directors has a fiduciary duty to undertake procedures that protect the interests of shareholders. Therefore, under a duty of care, the board of directors often relies on third-party financial advisors to independently provide advice as to the attractiveness of the offer. One data point often cited by the board and financial advisors is the relationship between the offer price and the historical trading range for the stock, most notably the 52-week high price. Such a price, although not necessarily a meaningful benchmark from a valuation perspective, nonetheless provides a data point that is easy to understand and communicate to shareholders and the investing public. In fact, a recent study of the linkage between psychological factors in transactions found that the relationship between the 52-week high price and the offer price was stronger than any of the other factors/independent variables considered.

In their paper "The Psychology of Pricing in Mergers and Acquisitions", Malcolm Baker, Xin Pan and Jeffrey Wurgler analyzed the impact of 52-week high prices on mergers and acquisitions activity. "Offer prices are highly influenced by the target's 52-week high stock price. This price likely serves as a psychological anchor – a starting point from which actual bid prices do not sufficiently adjust to reflect only current information. I show that the target's 52-week high exercises a strong effect on the bidder's offer price. A number of bidders offer exactly this price...The effect is difficult to square with alternative explanations and appears best explained in terms of the use of the 52-week high as a reference point by the target's shareholders or as an anchor in negotiations with the bidder." As described in the magazine *CFO*, "The study found that more deals were priced at that reference point than any other, and offers were more likely to be approved if they exceeded that high, even controlling for the level of the offer premium. In addition, the greater the difference between the 52-week high and the current stock price, the higher the premium that bidders paid for companies."[12]

The implication from the above study is that it may be prudent for valuation specialists to consider a 52-week stock price analysis of the seller companies included in control premium data search and, if publicly-traded, the subject company under analysis. All other considerations held constant, a trading price for the subject company near the 52-week high may imply the acceptability of a lower control premium while a trading price significantly below the 52-week high may imply the acceptability of a higher control premium. It may even be useful to consider calculating the value of a public guideline company or subject company by using its 52-week high stock price as a likely benchmark that financial advisory firms and board of directors would consult in preparing a bid or evaluating an offer. While certain databases, such as *Capital IQ*, include a data field such as "Percentage of 52-Week High", the results from the above research should perhaps lead this statistic to higher prominence among the numerous data points analyzed by valuation specialists.

Quantification of Control Premiums

An alternative to relying upon premiums paid from previous transactions is to focus solely on the attributes of the subject company. First, although valuation specialists generally assume that markets are efficient, there could be instances where a valuation specialist believes there is evidence that a subject company's stock is mispriced. To quote Warren Buffett, "I'd be a bum in the street if the markets were efficient."[13] The difficulty, of course, could be generating documentation to convince a reviewer that the markets are wrong. Assuming the subject company is publicly-traded, factors that *may* suggest that the subject company could be overvalued or undervalued (or at least increase the possibility of such an occurrence), include the following: low float, low trading volume, and lack of analyst coverage. Similarly, actions taken by management of the subject company, such as insider buying (selling) or stock buybacks (issuance), would indicate that management believes the subject company's stock is undervalued (overvalued). However, such bullish indicators by management do not guarantee that they are correct or that, if they are correct, the stock price will ever change to its *real* value.

12 Vincent Ryan, "Sellers High", *CFO* (July-August 2009), page 17.

13 Warren Buffett as quoted in *Fortune* (April 3, 1995).

Second, another approach could be considered that does not focus on the stock being mispriced, but rather focuses on a quantification of the potential synergies that a market participant may derive from acquiring the subject company.[14] In many instances, there may be less publicly-available data to model revenue synergies, but cost synergies are more easily modeled by examining elements of potential expense redundancies, such as executive compensation, and discussing the reasonableness of assumptions regarding the categories and magnitude of potential cost synergies with subject company management. In addition, research of prior relevant transactions may find categories and amounts related to synergy estimates, which may be discussed in press releases, investor presentations, and/or proxy statements. Once estimated, the present value of any synergies would be added to the stand-alone value of the subject company to calculate the *potential* value on a controlling interest basis. Finally, the valuation specialist must estimate the portion of the synergies that a hypothetical buyer would be willing to pay to/share with the seller shareholders. Although the track record for many acquisitions suggest that disproportionate value is often transferred from the shareholders of the buyer to the shareholders of the seller, a more practical approach would dictate a more conservative split of synergistic value between buyer and seller. Overall, if a control premium is being justified on the basis that a new owner/management would be able to increase value through either higher cash flows and/or lower cost of capital, then a valuation specialist should be prepared to be able to support how such value drivers could be achieved.

Conclusion

Control premiums are a significant input in many valuation engagements and are often featured prominently in assessing the reasonableness of an offer to acquire a public company. Significant data now exists that a valuation specialist may analyze in determining an appropriate control premium to apply. However, as discussed in this article, it appears that before determining what control premium to apply, the valuation specialist must answer a fundamental question: how to most meaningfully measure a control premium, in terms of equity or invested capital? The data presented in this article would appear to indicate that the utilization of invested capital is a more meaningful method of measuring a control premium and, therefore, applying a control premium to a public company value to convert it to a controlling interest basis. Other search criteria, such as buyer type, country, and exchange, indicated that these may also be important to consider in selecting transactions for further analysis. However, even if there is agreement by valuation specialists on the method of calculating a control premium and the criteria to utilize in selecting transactions, it is still a complex task to analyze transactions in order to consider the numerous factors that may have influenced the magnitude of the control premiums observed and then to relate these factors to a subject company at a different point in time with its own unique characteristics. Recent academic research has indicated that the 52-week high price for target companies has a key role in purchase prices and control premiums and, therefore, needs to be considered in a control premium analysis. Additional empirical study of control premium data may lead to a more meaningful analytical framework to be used by valuation specialists, financial advisory firms, and other interested constituents.

14 Lengthy discussion of this topic is included in "The Value of Synergy", white paper, Aswath Damodaran, (October 2005).

Bibliography

SEC Speeches

"SEC resists 'bright line rule' on control premiums – but still wants to see adequate support from appraisers." *BV Wire #77-1*, February 2009.

Robert G. Fox III, Professional Accounting Fellow, Office of the Chief Accountant U.S. Securities and Exchange Commission, Speech to the 2008 AICPA National Conference on Current SEC and PCAOB Developments, December 8, 2008. http://www.sec.gov/news/speech/2008/spch120808rgf.htm

SEC Comment Letters

http://www.sec.gov/answers/edgarletters.htm

The Appraisal Foundation Control Premium Working Group

See website for documents posted and public comments. https://netforum.avectra.com/eWeb/DynamicPage.aspx?Site=TAF&WebCode=EDVFR

Use of Control Premiums in Fairness Opinions
Philip J. Clements and Philip W. Wisler, *The Standard & Poor's Guide to Fairness Opinions: A User's Guide for Fiduciaries* (2005).

Estimates of Value from Synergy
"The Value of Synergy", white paper, Aswath Damodaran, (October 2005).

Estimates of Value from Control
"The Value of Control: Implications for Control Premia, Minority Discounts and Voting Share Differentials", white paper, Aswath Damodaran, (June 2005).

Z. Christopher Mercer and Travis Harms, *Business Valuation: An Integrated Theory*, John Wiley & Sons (2008).

Behavioral Factors Influencing Offer Prices
Vincent Ryan, "Sellers High", *CFO* (July-August 2009), page 17.

"The Psychology of Pricing in Mergers and Acquisitions", white paper, Malcolm Baker, Xin Pan and Jeffrey Wurgler.

Management Hubris
Richard Roll, "The Hubris Hypothesis of Corporate Takeovers," *Journal of Business* 59, no. 2 (1986): 212.

Matthew L.A. Hayward and Donald C. Hambrick, "Explaining Premiums Paid for Large Acquisitions: Evidence of CEO Hubris," New York: Columbia University Graduate School of Business (June 1995).

Quantitative Analysis of Control Premium Data
Brad Pursel, "Control Premiums: Application and Analysis", *Business Valuation Update*, March 2010.

"The Value of Control: Implications for Control Premia, Minority Discounts and Voting Share Differentials", white paper, Aswath Damodaran, (June 2005). See paper for various citations.

Dan Jordan and Paul Hoppe, "Is the Mergerstat Control Premium Overstated?" *Journal of Business Valuation and Economic Loss Analysis*, Volume 3, Issue 1, 2008.

Papers Questioning Applicability of Control Premiums
"The Fair Value of Cornfields in Delaware Appraisal Law", Lawrence A. Hamermesh and Michael L. Wachter, *Journal of Corporation Law*, Fall 2005.

"A Review of Valuations in Delaware Appraisal Cases, 2004-2005", Gilbert E. Matthews, *Business Valuation Review*, June 2006.

"Misuse of Control Premiums in Delaware Appraisals", Gilbert E. Matthews, *Business Valuation Review*, October, 2008.

"Implied Minority Discounts in Statutory Fair Value: The Doctrine that Just Won't Die", Gilbert E. Matthews and Michael Wachter, *Business Valuation Update*, December, 2009

"Implied minority discount lacks theoretical, financial basis", *BVWire*™, October 21, 2009

"Control Premiums and Minority Discounts: The Need for Specific Economic Analysis", Mark Lee, *Business Valuation Update*, August, 2001.

"Control Premium High Jinks", Eric Nath and Mark Lee, Presentation to the American Society of Appraisers, International Conference, 2003

Relevant BVR Teleconferences
Control Premia Teleconference Transcript, August 24, 2006, Aswath Damodaran, Kenneth Woo and Anna Berhelius.

Implied Minority Discounts in Statutory Fair Value: The Doctrine that Just Won't Die, March 19, 2010, Gilbert E. Matthews and Michael Wachter.

General Overview
Shannon Pratt, *Business Valuation Discounts and Premiums*, John Wiley & Sons, Second Edition (2009).

Misuse of Control Premiums in Delaware Appraisals

by Gilbert E. Matthews, CFA

In statutory appraisal cases, Delaware Courts sometimes apply premiums that are based on questionable reasoning. They commonly adjust guideline company valuations for an "implicit minority discount", they apply acquisition premiums to subsidiaries, and they often rely upon average premiums in acquisitions as a basis for calculating control premiums. This article discusses the flaws in the reasoning underlying these adjustments.

Introduction

Delaware corporate law is preeminent in establishing standards for corporate valuations because a majority of publicly traded companies are incorporated in Delaware. Valuations in numerous dissenting shareholder appraisals have been adjudicated under the Delaware appraisal statute. The appraisal statute states that "the Court shall determine the fair value of the shares exclusive of any element of value arising from the accomplishment or expectation of the merger or consolidation" giving rise to the appraisal proceeding.[1] A large body of Delaware case law has developed interpreting the statute's mandate to "determine the fair value of the shares" in Delaware dissenting shareholder cases. The result is that the fair value standard for the subject company's value is to be ascertained on a "going-concern" basis:

> [F]or many decades, the Delaware courts have embraced a standard of valuation in appraisal cases that awards dissenting stockholders their proportional share of the value of the "going concern."[2]

In this article, we address the Delaware courts' use of control premiums in appraisal cases and explain why both the underlying theory and resulting practice are no longer valid. In three important legal articles, the courts' application of control premiums has been criticized for deviating from going-concern value. The first, by Professor Richard Booth (University of Maryland School of Law)[3] in 2001, was followed in 2003 by an article by Professor William Carney (Emory University School of Law) and Mark Heimendinger (Milbank, Tweed, Hadley & McCloy).[4] The most recent work is a thoughtful and thorough law review article by Professors Lawrence Hamermesh (Widener University School of Law) and Michael Wachter (University of Pennsylvania Law School).[5]

This article continues the questioning of the Delaware courts' use of control premiums, but from a business valuation perspective. This author has been addressing these issues for more than a decade,[6] but commentators have expanded the dialogue in the last few years. This article will attempt to incorporate their ideas as it discusses three concepts concerning the application of control premiums that Delaware Courts have adopted:

1 8 Del. Code Ann. tit. 8, §262(h).

2 Lawrence A. Hamermesh and Michael L. Wachter, "The Short and Puzzling Life of the 'Implicit Minority Discount' in Delaware Appraisal Law," 156 U. Pa. L. Rev. 1 (2007), pp. 3–4. Professor Hamermesh, a prominent commentator on Delaware law, was a partner of a major Delaware firm and litigated appraisal cases.

3 Richard A. Booth, "Minority Discounts and Control Premiums in Appraisal Proceedings," 57 Business Lawyer 127 (2001).

4 William J. Carney and Mark Heimendinger, "Appraising the Nonexistent: The Delaware Courts' Struggle with Control Premiums," 152 U. Pa. L. Rev. 845 (2003).

5 Lawrence A. Hamermesh and Michael L. Wachter, "The Short and Puzzling Life."

6 Several of the writer's relevant publications are cited herein.

This article first appeared in the Summer 2008 Edition of Business Valuation Review. Copyright 2008, American Society of Appraisers. Reprinted with permission.

- The concept that market prices of shares include an inherent minority discount, thereby requiring the Court's addition of a control premium to valuations that are based on guideline companies;

- The concept that a subsidiary of a company should be valued by adding a control premium to reflect the parent's control of its subsidiaries; and

- The concept that it is appropriate to take average acquisition premiums and apply them to guideline companies that are not acquisition targets, as well as to subsidiaries of subject companies.

The Delaware courts have unfortunately accepted the concept that guideline company valuations in appraisal cases should be adjusted upward to offset an implicit minority discount (IMD).[7] They have done so based on both expert witness testimony and the mid-1990s writings of well-respected authors who have since changed their views. Since 1995, the Chancery Court has added a control premium to offset the IMD in a substantial majority of the decisions in which it relied on guideline companies. In fact, in every case where petitioner's expert adjusted for an IMD, the Court accepted the concept. The Court's preference for IMD adjustments is illustrated in the following Delaware appraisal decision where, in fact, *neither* expert's valuation included an IMD, but the Court felt constrained by "precedent" to apply it.

> Delaware law recognizes that there is an inherent minority trading discount in a comparable company analysis because "the valuation method depends on comparisons to market multiples derived from trading information for minority blocks of the comparable companies." The equity valuation produced in a comparable company analysis does not accurately reflect the intrinsic worth of a corporation on a going-concern basis. Therefore, the court, in appraising the fair value of the equity, "must correct this minority trading discount by adding back a premium designed to correct it." ... [T]he recent appraisal cases that correct the valuation for a minority discount by adding back a premium "that spreads the value of control over all shares equally consistently use a 30% adjustment. *Relying on recent precedents,* the court will adjust the ... per share value by adding a 30% control premium" [*emphasis added*].[8]

The regrettable result is that the Court ends up adjusting guideline company valuations based on its questionable concept that market prices of publicly traded companies bear an implicit minority discount and therefore are inherently "undervalued."

The components of the Court's IMD theory are that:

(a) publicly traded companies' shares trade below their pro rata portion of going-concern value;

(b) they do so because these shares trade below financial control value, so that

(c) it is necessary for the court to add a "control premium" to valuations based on guideline companies.

Because most acquisitions of control of public companies are at share prices above market, the Chancery Court erroneously concludes that shares of all public companies are generally trading below their control value. In order to compensate for this perceived undervaluation in appraisal cases, the Court adds a premium when applying the guideline company method. The Court determines the size of the control premium for companies (or in some cases, subsidiaries) by reference to the average premiums over market paid in acquisitions. This article explains why both the theory and practice are wrong.

Control Premiums and Levels of Value

Any discussion of control premiums must begin with a discussion of "levels of value," a model that has evolved over the past eighteen years as a result of the financial community's thinking. The model is presented and explained by two leading valuation authorities in recent editions of their books:

7 The IMD is sometimes called an "inherent minority discount" or an "implied minority discount."

8 *Doft & Co., Inc. v. Travelocity.com, Inc.,* 2004 Del. Ch. LEXIS 75 (May 21, 2004) at *45–*47 [footnotes omitted].

Shannon Pratt's Valuing a Business[9] and Z. Christopher Mercer's *Business Valuation: An Integrated Theory.*[10]

Pratt's levels of value chart shows five levels of value for publicly traded companies: synergistic (strategic) value, value of control shares, market value of freely traded minority shares, value of restricted stock, and value of nonmarketable shares.[11] The latter two levels are not relevant in a Delaware appraisal because marketability discounts are not permitted under Delaware law.

Mercer illustrates the levels of value in Figure 1.[12] In this diagram, Strategic Control Value (Pratt's "synergistic value") is the business's value to a party that could achieve synergistic benefits if it had control. Financial Control Value (Pratt's "value of control shares") does not include anticipated synergies, but includes "the ability of a specific buyer to improve the existing operations or run the target company more efficiently."[13] Marketable Minority Value is the market value of freely traded minority shares.[14]

Under Delaware case law, companies must be appraised on an "as is" basis. A Delaware appraisal values a company as a going concern based on the way it is being managed at the time of the valuation—a concept called "operative reality." Going-concern value based on operative reality does not include potential benefits such as cost savings that an acquirer may achieve, such as eliminating the costs of being a public company or reducing excessive management compensation.

Figure 1: Levels of Value

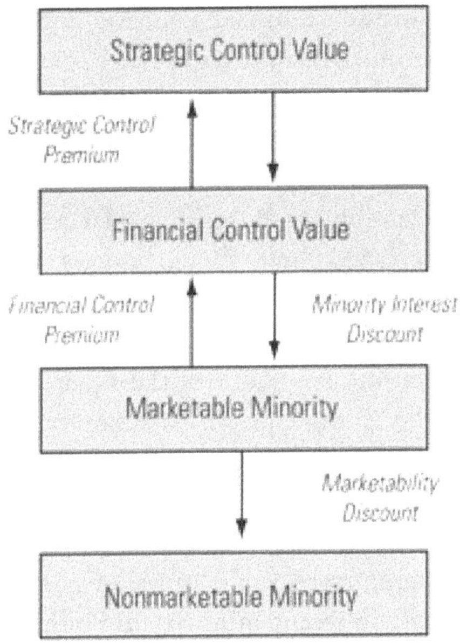

> The company, with all of its warts and diamonds, is valued in terms of the discounted free cash flow generated by the company's assets and reinvestment opportunities. In measuring the value of the warts and diamonds, the warts are valued as warts and the diamonds as diamonds. The minority shareholders cannot claim that if the company were run differently, or if it were owned by a third-party, the warts would become diamonds. That may be correct as a factual matter, but is irrelevant to the issue. The minority's claim is equal to the value of the shares into the future, and that value is a mix of the existing warts and diamonds.
>
> Similarly, the controller cannot claim that the diamonds are really warts. More specifically, if the company already has reinvestment plans that would fix current problems in the future, the value of those plans are part of the value of the company as an operating concern.[15]

Delaware appraisal value generally would equal Marketable Minority Value. In situations when market prices are depressed and shares trade below their going-concern value, then the going-concern value of a company under Delaware

9 Shannon P. Pratt, *Valuing a Business: The Analysis and Appraisal of Closely Held Companies.* 5th ed. (New York: McGraw-Hill, 2008).

10 Z. Christopher Mercer and Travis W. Harms. 2007, *Business Valuation: An Integrated Theory.* 2nd ed. (New York: Wiley, 2007).

11 Pratt, *op. cit.,* p. 384. The restricted stock level is for shares that are not currently marketable but will become marketable with the passage of time.

12 Mercer and Harms, p. 71. Mercer's current view as to the relationship between Marketable Minority Value and Financial Control Value is discussed later in this article.

13 *Id.,* p. 73.

14 As discussed in detail later in this article, (a) publicly traded shares may trade at prices higher or lower than Financial Control Value, and may even sometimes trade above Strategic Control Value, and (b) many commentators believe that most actively traded shares are usually priced close to Financial Control Value.

15 Hamermesh and Wachter, "The Fair Value of Cornfields in Delaware Appraisal Law," 31 J. Corp. Law 119 (2005), pp. 143–144.

appraisal law would be higher than Marketable Minority Value. In situations where there are any cost savings available to an acquiror, the going-concern value of the company being appraised would be lower than Financial Control Value. If the expert believes that going-concern value in a particular situation is not equal to Marketable Minority Value, the expert's testimony should address the market and financial factors that justify the conclusion.

Although Delaware law requires the Court to find value according to the "going-concern" standard of fair value, the Court is, in fact, currently using two different levels of value depending on which valuation method it elects to employ. When the Court uses the guideline company method to calculate going-concern value and adjusts for IMD, it is determining the inherent minority discount by reference to premiums paid in acquisitions (excluding synergies). Thus, the guideline company valuation that results from the Court's addition of a control premium to offset the IMD is, in fact, Financial Control Value.

In contrast, when the Court uses the discounted cash flow method to calculate going-concern value based on operative reality (which excludes cost savings that a financial buyer might consider), it calculates Marketable Minority Value. There is no dispute in Delaware that the projections used in a DCF valuation cannot be adjusted for changes that an existing management does not intend to undertake. Under Delaware law, no adjustments are permitted for changes that might be made by a new control shareholder, and the company must be valued as a going concern as it is being run by existing management. Thus, a Delaware Court's going-concern DCF valuations arrive at a different level of value than its guideline company valuations adjusted for IMD.

In Delaware, "control premium" has more than one meaning

The Court uses the term "control premium" to describe three different premiums. To the extent that the Court concludes that market prices of publicly traded shares include a minority discount, it makes an adjustment by adding a "control premium" to arrive at its determination of going-concern value (fair value). Here, the term "control premium," as used by the Court for this adjustment, is the premium that Mercer's diagram calls the "Financial Control Premium"—it is the inverse of the diminution in market price attributable to IMD. The Court usually bases its determination on testimony as to average premiums in acquisitions; it makes an adjustment to eliminate the impact of synergies and then applies this "control premium" to offset a perceived minority discount in valuations based on guideline companies.

Confusingly, however, Delaware decisions have also used the phrase "control premium" with two other meanings. The phrase has been used by the Court of Chancery not only to describe the inverse of the minority discount, but also to portray the premium above the Financial Control Value that would be paid by a synergistic buyer for control of a company.[16] This premium— the Strategic Control Premium—is impermissible in a Delaware appraisal (except, inexplicably, in valuing subsidiaries of holding companies, as discussed below).

In addition, the Court has used the term "control premium" in yet a third way: to describe the sum of the Financial Control Premium and the Strategic Control Premium.[17] This premium, the difference between Marketable Minority Value and Strategic Control Value, is more accurately known as the "acquisition premium."[18] It is the difference between the market prices of shares prior to a transaction and the price paid for the shares in a change-of-control transaction, and it includes the premium, if any, paid for synergies. These acquisition premiums are the data points published in sources such as *Mergerstat Review* that are commonly used by testifying experts. This is the only premium that is directly observable in the market, so that it becomes necessary for experts and the Court to estimate (or speculate) as to the portion attributable to synergies.

The Delaware courts could avoid the "control premium" ambiguity by using the levels-of-value model and the terminology developed by the financial community. The Court could then conceptualize and use the terms "Financial Control Premium" and "Strategic Control Premium" as in

16 *E.g., Le Beau v. M.G. Bancorp., Inc.,* 1998 Del. Ch. LEXIS 9 (Jan. 29, 1998), aff'd *M.G. Bancorp., Inc. v. Le Beau,* 737 A.2d 513 (Del. 1999).

17 *E.g., Agranoff v. Miller,* 791 A.2d 880 (Del. Ch. 2001) at 899.

18 Pratt, Business Valuation Discounts and Premiums (New York: Wiley, 2001), 60; Pratt, Valuing a Business, 5th ed. (2008), 384.

the diagram above, and employ "Acquisition Premium" to describe the difference between Marketable Minority Value and Strategic Control Value. If the Court, authors, and expert witnesses shared a common and consistent language, they could concentrate with greater precision on any true differences in the appraisal valuation.

The Court adds premium for change of control to values of subsidiaries

The Delaware Supreme Court opened the door to a use of premiums for change of control in *Rapid American* in 1992, when it applied premiums to valuations of subsidiaries.[19] Rapid American was a holding company whose three subsidiaries operated in widely different industries. The trial court had valued each subsidiary based solely on guideline companies. The Delaware Supreme Court concluded that the lower court had effectively "treated Rapid as a minority shareholder in its wholly-owned subsidiaries" because the market prices of the guideline companies "do not reflect a control premium."[20] Its reasoning was that the inherent value of the parent holding company included the control value of the 100 percent–owned subsidiaries.[21]

On remand, the trial court applied acquisition premiums (called "control premiums" in the decision) of 45%, 20%, and 30% to the three subsidiaries, which were the average premiums paid in acquisitions in the subsidiaries' respective industries as determined by petitioners' expert.[22] The Chancery Court did not indicate whether it had reduced these average acquisition premiums for synergies, so that these control premiums apparently increased the valuation of the subsidiaries to the Strategic Control Value level. This ambiguity illustrates the confusion caused by the failure of expert witnesses and the Courts to clarify the meaning of "control premium" and to specify the level of value being discussed.

19 *Harris v. Rapid-American Corp.,* 603 A.2d 796 (Del. 1992), reversing the denial of control premiums in *Harris v. Rapid-American Corp.,* 1990 Del. Ch. LEXIS 166 (Oct. 2, 1990) and remanding the case.

20 Id. at 804.

21 Id. at 804.

22 *Harris v. Rapid-American Corp.,* 1992 Del. Ch. LEXIS 75 (Apr. 1, 1992). The unaffected market price of Rapid-American had been $17.25 per share, the going-private consideration (primarily in debentures) was worth approximately $28 per share, the initial appraisal value was $51 per share, and the ultimate appraisal with the control premiums was $73.29 per share.

The IMD enters Delaware case law

The IMD was first considered (and rejected) by the Court of Chancery in 1991, when plaintiff's expert in Radiology argued that her DCF valuation should be adjusted upward by 30% to eliminate an implicit minority discount.[23] The Court rejected this adjustment, stating, "The discounted cash flow method purports to represent the present value of Radiology's cash flow. ... The discounted cash flow analysis, as employed in this case, fully reflects this value without need for an adjustment."[24]

The application of an IMD to a guideline company valuation was rejected shortly afterwards in a valuation of Interstate Bakeries.[25] The respondent's expert disputed the petitioner's expert's contention that market value of publicly traded companies "is inevitably less than intrinsic value"[26] and the Court rejected the petitioner's position.

Later in 1992, the Court of Chancery accepted an IMD for the first time in *Spectrum Technology,* where the expert for the respondent (who had unsuccessfully argued for an IMD as plaintiff's witness in *Radiology*) added a 30% adjustment for IMD to her guideline company valuation, even though she was working for the side that logically should have argued for a lower value.[27] Hamermesh and Wachter commented:

> [Her testimony] of course met no opposition from the petitioner, and the court did not reject the adjustment sua sponte. To the contrary, the adjustment was incorporated in the final valuation result without comment or evaluation by the Vice Chancellor. Thus, the IMD was first planted in Delaware valuation doctrine not by adversarial process and judicial evaluation, but by default.[28]

23 *In re Radiology Associates,* A.2d 485 (Del. Ch. 1991).

24 *Id.* at 494.

25 *Salomon Bros. v. Interstate Bakeries Corp.,* 1992 Del. Ch. LEXIS 100 (May 1, 1992).

26 *Id.* at *15.

27 *Hodas v. Spectrum Technology, Inc.,* 1992 Del. Ch. LEXIS 252 (Dec. 7, 1992).

28 Hamermesh and Wachter, "The Short and Puzzling Life," pp. 18–19.

The Vice Chancellor did not explicitly discuss an IMD, but a review of the Court's valuation demonstrates that it included an adjustment for IMD.[29]

The Court's next appraisal using a guideline company analysis was *Kleinwort Benson Ltd. v. Silgan Corp.*[30] in 1995. Here the petitioner's expert added an 86% premium. The Court-appointed expert testified that "the premium necessary to remove the minority discount inherent in publicly traded stock is somewhere between zero and the control premium which [petitioner's expert's] study places between 34–48%."[31] Although Silgan Corp. argued that no reliable proof of an IMD had been presented, its own expert testified that it was reasonable to use a minority discount of 10–15%. The Court, noting respondent's expert's accord on the IMD issue, used the midpoint of his range and applied a 12.5% adjustment.[32] The Court noted that it had rejected an IMD in valuing Interstate Bakeries, but explained that "our different conclusions result from differences in the records [i.e., the testimony] presented by the parties in the respective cases."[33]

The Court again adds control premiums to valuations of subsidiaries

In two 1998 cases, *M.G. Bancorp. and Hintmann,*[34] the Court, relying on *Rapid-American,* added control premiums to valuations of subsidiaries in which the experts used the guideline company method. (This writer criticized these adjustments at the time.[35])

The Chancery Court rejected the respondents' guideline company valuation of M.G. Bancorporation, a holding company with two bank subsidiaries, because the Vice Chancellor concluded that respondents' valuation did not adjust for an IMD. He pointed out that a book co-authored by respondents' expert Robert Reilly (the then-current 3rd Edition of *Valuing a Business*) supported the position that guideline companies include a minority discount.[36] The Court also cited Christopher Mercer's *Valuing Financial Institutions* on this point.[37]

The Court based its valuation of M.G. Bancorporation on guideline *transactions* (a method usually rejected in Delaware appraisals), thereby effectively including an acquisition premium and valuing the subsidiaries at the Strategic Control Level. The Court followed *Rapid-American* in reasoning that, since the parent controlled its two bank subsidiaries, acquisition value was an appropriate measure. The respondent unsuccessfully argued that although *Rapid-American* permitted premiums in valuing subsidiaries, it applied only to conglomerates, not to a single-industry holding company. The Supreme Court upheld the lower court's decision to apply acquisition premiums to the bank subsidiaries.

The trial court in *Hintmann* treated the company as a holding company even though it operated primarily through a single subsidiary. Petitioners' expert found that the mean and median acquisition premiums for publicly held companies were 45% and 55%, respectively. The Court adjusted the premium down to 20% to eliminate synergies, and it applied the 20% premium to the mean of the guideline company and DCF values.[38] No prior or subsequent appraisal decision has applied a control premium to a discounted cash flow valuation (see discussion *infra*), but the Chancery Court has continued to apply premiums to guideline company valuations.

---

29 Professor Hamermesh, who was counsel for respondent in *Hodas,* has kindly clarified the Court's calculations in correspondence with the writer.

30 1995 Del. Ch. LEXIS 75 (June 15, 1995).

31 *Id.* at *11–12.

32 *Id.* at *12. It is not clear from the decision whether the Court added a 12.5% premium or adjusted for a 12.5% discount (i.e., added a 14.3% premium).

33 *Id.* at *9.

34 *Hintmann v. Fred Weber, Inc.,* 1998 Del. Ch. LEXIS 26 (Feb 17, 1998).

35 Gilbert E. Matthews, "Delaware Court Relies on Comparable Acquisition Method: *LeBeau v. M.G. Bancorporation, Inc.,*" *Business Valuation Update,* March 1998; Matthews, "Delaware Court Adds Control Premium to Subsidiary Value: *Hintmann v. Fred Weber, Inc.,*" *Business Valuation Update,* May 1998.

36 *Le Beau* at *25, citing Shannon P. Pratt, Robert F. Reilly, and Robert P. Schweihs, *Valuing a Business: The Analysis and Appraisal of Closely Held Companies,* 3rd ed. (Irwin, 1996), 194–195 and 210.

37 Z. Christopher Mercer, *Valuing Financial Institutions* (Irwin, 1992), 198–200 and Ch. 13.

38 *Hintmann* at *31.

The Court applies an adjustment for IMD—but not always

In the decade since the Chancery Court's decisions in *M.G. Bancorp. and Hintmann,* it has repeatedly demonstrated its acceptance of the IMD concept, commonly using a 30% premium. Whenever the dissenting shareholders' expert adjusted for an IMD, the Court did so as well. In one decision (*Prescott,* discussed below), the Court added a premium to offset IMD over the respondent's objection.[39] Indeed, in one case (*Doft,* quoted in the opening section of this article), the Court added a premium even though neither expert did so (see further discussion below).

The Court has chosen to use the guideline company method in approximately half of its valuations under the Delaware appraisal standard,[40] and it has adjusted for IMD in nine of those 14 decisions (including *Prescott* and *Doft*). These cases are briefly discussed below. In five cases in which an IMD adjustment was not included in either side's valuations, the Court applied no premium.[41] The seven cases where respondents did not object to the IMD concept are:

- *Borruso:*[42] Both experts used a 30% control premium to offset IMD, and the Court adopted that figure.[43] The Court wrote that "the comparable company method of analysis produces an equity valuation that inherently reflects a minority discount, as the data used for purposes of comparison is all derived from minority trading values of the comparable companies." [44]
- *Bomarko:*[45] The Court accepted plaintiffs' expert's 30% adjustment to offset IMD. The defendants' expert conceded that a guideline company analysis reflects an IMD, but argued unsuccessfully that no party would pay a premium to acquire the troubled subject company.[46]
- *Agranoff:* In calculating fair value, the Court again made a 30% adjustment for IMD, lower than plaintiffs' expert and higher than defendants' expert.[47] The Court's comments were similar to those in *Borruso:* "The comparable companies' analysis generates an equity value that includes an inherent minority trading discount, because the method depends on comparisons to market multiples derived from trading information for minority blocks of the comparable companies."[48]
- *Lane v. Cancer Treatment Centers:*[49] The Court's guideline company valuation adopted petitioner's expert's 20% premium to offset IMD.[50] Respondent's expert did not discuss IMD because he valued the company at zero.[51]
- *Dobler v. Montgomery Cellular:*[52] The Court accepted the 31% premium used by the dissenting shareholders' expert in his guideline company analysis, which was slightly less than the premium used by company's expert.[53]

39 *Prescott Group Small Cap, L.P. v. Coleman Co.,* 2004 Del. Ch. LEXIS 131 (Sept. 8, 2004).

40 The Court has utilized DCF in most of its appraisal valuations. In some cases, the guideline company method was not used by the experts, and in some the Court rejected an expert's guideline company valuation.

41 *Gonsalves v. Straight Arrow Publishers, Inc.,* 1996 Del. Ch. LEXIS 144 (Nov. 27, 1996), rev'd in part 701 A.2d 357 (Del. 1997), 793 A.2d 312 (Del. Ch 1998), rev'd in part 1999 Del. LEXIS (Jan. 5, 1999), 2002 Del. Ch. LEXIS 105 (Sept. 10, 2002); *Gray v. Cytokine Pharmasciences, Inc,* 2002 Del. Ch. LEXIS 48 (Apr. 25, 2002); *Gentile v. SinglePoint Financial, Inc.,* 2003 Del. Ch. LEXIS 21 (Mar. 5, 2003). *Taylor v. American Specialty Retailing Group, Inc.,* 2003 Del. Ch. LEXIS 75 (July 25, 2003); *In re U.S. Cellular Operating Co.,* 2005 Del. Ch. LEXIS 1 (Jan. 6, 2005).

42 *Borruso v. Communications Telesystems International,* 753 A.2d 451 (Del. Ch. 1999).

43 *Id.* at 457–458.

44 *Id.* at 458.

45 *Bomarko, Inc. v. International Telecharge, Inc.,* 794 A.2d 1161 (Del. Ch. 1999), aff'd. *International Telecharge, Inc. v. Bomarko,* 766 A.2d 437 (Del. 2000).

46 *Id.* at 1186–1187.

47 *Agranoff* at 900.

48 *Id.* at 892.

49 *Lane v. Cancer Treatment Centers of America, Inc.,* 2004 Del. Ch. LEXIS 108 (July 30, 2004).

50 *Id.* at *130.

51 *Id.* at *33.

52 *Dobler v. Montgomery Cellular Holding Co.,* 2004 Del. Ch. LEXIS 139 (Oct. 4, 2004), aff'd. *Montgomery Cellular Holding Co. v. Dobler,* 880 A.2d 206 (Del. 2005).

53 *Id.* at *16, *67. The Court gave a 65% weight to guideline transactions, 30% to discounted cash flow, and only 5% to guideline companies. *Id.* at *73. The unusual weight given to guideline transactions reflected the fact that the principal guideline transaction was a proposed acquisition of a group of companies that included Montgomery Cellular itself. *Id.* at *60–63.

- *Andaloro:*[54] The Court applied a 30% control premium to offset IMD, reducing the 38% premium used by defendant's expert because that figure did not "exclude any portion of the average premia from his sample to account for the sharing of synergies by the buyer with the seller." [55]

- *Highfields Capital:*[56] Petitioner's expert used a 30.1% adjustment for IMD and respondent's expert used 16.1% in their valuations of The MONY Group. The Court accepted the respondent's expert's guideline company valuation of MONY's asset management business, including his 16.1% adjustment.[57] (Although MONY was a holding company, the decision did not address adding control premiums to valuations of its subsidiaries.)

In the one appraisal where the Court added a control premium in spite of respondent's objection, the Court's reprimand to respondent clearly conveyed its adherence to the orthodoxy of the IMD concept. In *Prescott,* respondent argued that the adjustment adding a control premium was inadmissible under Delaware law. The Court not only rejected respondent's argument, but admonished, "This argument runs so blatantly counter to the *settled Delaware precedent* on the subject ... as to call into question Coleman's good faith in advancing it" [*emphasis added*].[58] Petitioner's expert's added a 35% premium to eliminate IMD in its guideline company valuation[59] and the Court ruled that this adjustment was consistent with Delaware law.[60]

In *Doft,* an extreme example of the Court's acceptance of the IMD concept, it made an arbitrary adjustment for IMD even though neither expert had even mentioned IMD in his report. The decision discussed the investment banker's fairness opinion presentation showing that the average premium in minority squeeze-outs was 50%, but noted that Travelocity.com was not directly comparable to any of the companies in those minority squeeze-out transactions.[61] The Court cited *Agranoff, Bomarko,* and *Borruso* and applied the often-used 30% adjustment for IMD.[62]

The Court has not applied IMD to DCF valuations—except once

The view that the DCF value of a company should not be adjusted for a control premium is consistent with generally accepted practice in the financial community. Pratt explains that a DCF value based on projected cash flows does not require the addition of a control premium.[63] For a Delaware appraisal, the relevant projections are those prepared by management, and dissenting shareholders are entitled to their pro rata share of the valuation based on management projections which do not include changes that a third party might make.

Only the *Hintmann* case (discussed above) has applied a premium to a discounted cash flow valuation. The *Hintmann* decision did not discuss why the Court believed that a premium should be added to DCF value. This is an aberrant and illogical holding, inconsistent both with other cases and with valuation practice. *Hintmann* did not discuss whether terminal value had been calculated using a multiple or a growth model.

Although Delaware has adjusted guideline company valuations for IMD on numerous occasions (as discussed previously), they have never applied a control premium to a terminal value calculated by using multiples derived from guideline companies. A control premium on terminal value was rejected in 1991 in *Radiology Associates.* Subsequently, the Court has used multiples to calculate terminal value in

54 *Andaloro v. PFPC Worldwide, Inc.,* 2005 Del. Ch. LEXIS 125 (Aug. 19, 2005).

55 *Id.* at *69. The Court applied the premium to equity value, rejecting plaintiff's overreaching claim that it should apply to enterprise value including debt.

56 *Highfields Capital, Ltd. v. AXA Financial, Inc.,* 2007 Del. Ch. LEXIS 126 (June 27, 2007).

57 *Id.* at 45.

58 *Prescott* at *99.

59 *Id.* at *90.

60 *Id.* at *99–100.

61 *Doft* at *46. 62 63 64 *Gilbert v. MPM Enterprises,* 709 A.2d 663 (Del. Ch. 1997); Gray v. Cytokine Pharmasciences, Inc. 2002 Del. Ch. LEXIS 48 (Apr. 25, 2002); In re U.S. Cellular Operating Co., 2005 Del Ch. LEXIS 1 (Jan. 6, 2005).

62 *Id.* at *46–47.

63 Pratt, *Business Valuation Discounts and Premiums* (2001), 30; Pratt, *Valuing a Business,* 5th ed. (2008), 228. Pratt points out that a DCF value not based on a control party's projections may not reflect control value.

four appraisal opinions, but no premiums were proposed by petitioners' experts in any of these cases.[64]

However, there is an inconsistency between adjusting for IMD in guideline company valuations and not adjusting terminal values based on multiples derived from guideline companies. The Court's first recognition of this contradiction was in 2006, when the Court stated that "an exit multiple based on minority trading data ... [is] a less favored technique [for determining terminal value] that raises questions about whether it embeds a minority discount."[65] This point was addressed by Hamermesh and Wachter, who argued that any adjustments for IMD were improper:

> [T]he Delaware courts' application of the IMD has rendered their valuation jurisprudence internally inconsistent. Even as they have recently come to insist on adjusting for the putative IMD when using a [guideline company approach], the Delaware courts have consistently (and properly) declined to make any such upward adjustment to the results of discounted cash flow (DCF) analysis.[66]

Hamermesh and Wachter noted, "It appears that Vice Chancellor Strine, the author of the *PNB Holding* opinion, has recognized the inconsistency we point out."[67]

It is undisputed in Delaware that no premium should be applied when terminal value is determined using a growth model (the academically preferred approach). Premiums to DCF valuations using growth models were explicitly rejected in 2004 in both *Dobler* and *Cancer Treatment Centers,* even though the Court adjusted for IMD in its guideline company valuations in both cases.[68] The Court in *Dobler,* citing Pratt's *Lawyer's Business Valuation Handbook,* said:

> [DCF] value should represent the full value of the future cash flows of the business. Excluding synergies, a company cannot be worth a premium over the value of its future cash flows. Thus, it is improper and illogical to add a control premium to a DCF valuation.[69]

It added, "A DCF is a final valuation that does not need any additional correction, such as a control premium."[70] The Court in *Cancer Treatment Centers* expressed this virtually unanimous position when it discussed DCF valuation: "The streams of income here do not require any adjustment for an impermissible minority discount."[71]

The Misuse of Control Premiums

The balance of this article comments on the conceptual errors that have crept into Delaware's application of control premiums in appraisals, both in valuing subsidiaries of holding companies and in adjusting for implied minority discounts. It also addresses a related issue—the misuse of average acquisition premiums.

Is a business worth more if it is a subsidiary?

The Delaware Supreme Court has approved the valuations of subsidiaries at a Strategic Control Level (thus including synergistic premiums), even though they do not permit operating companies to be valued at the same level. For operating companies, we have seen that the Court mistakenly adjusts for an assumed IMD, which results in appraisal values being increased by the Court's "control" augmentation. For subsidiaries, however, the Court leapfrogs higher and awards a "strategic" or "synergistic" premium.

The Supreme Court valuations approved in *Rapid-American* and *M.G. Bancorp.* were arrived at by applying average premiums in acquisition transactions to the calculated values of the subsidiaries with no adjustments to eliminate the

64 *Gilbert v. MPM Enterprises,* 709 A.2d 663 (Del. Ch. 1997); *Gray v. Cytokine Pharmasciences, Inc.* 2002 Del. Ch. LEXIS 48 (Apr. 25, 2002); *In re U.S. Cellular Operating Co.,* 2005 Del Ch. LEXIS 1 (Jan. 6, 2005).

65 *In re PNB Holding Co. Shareholders Litigation,* 2006 Del. Ch. LEXIS 158 (Aug. 18, 2006) at *114–*115. The Court chose to use respondent's growth model rather than petitioner's exit multiple for determining terminal value.

66 Hamermesh and Wachter, "The Short and Puzzling Life," p. 6.

67 *Id.,* p. 6, footnote 19.

68 *Dobler* at *72 and *65–*66; Lane v. Cancer Treatment Centers at *117–118 and *129.

69 Pratt, *The Lawyer's Business Valuation Handbook* (American Bar Association, 2000), 359, quoting Matthews, "Delaware Court Adds Control Premium to Subsidiary Value."

70 *Dobler* at *72.

71 *Lane v. Cancer Treatment Centers* at *117–*118.

effect of synergies on the data. The result thus represents the Strategic Control level of value. The average premiums necessarily derive from acquisition prices that include potential synergies. Synergies can only be realized upon completion of a transaction. Thus, the Court's use of acquisition values appears to be contrary to the appraisal statute's mandate that "the Court shall determine the fair value of the shares exclusive of any element of value arising from the accomplishment or expectation of the merger or consolidation."[72]

The premium that was added in *Hintmann* to the wholly owned subsidiary would not have been added if the business had been a division. However, the value of an operating business is not increased if it operates as an incorporated subsidiary of a corporate parent rather than as a division or, indeed, as the sole operating business of the company being appraised. In 2001 Vice Chancellor Leo Strine recognized this anomaly:

> It seems a fine point to conclude that the value of the entity as a going concern includes the potential to sell controlled subsidiaries for a premium but not the potential to sell the entity itself.[73]

Professors Hamermesh and Wachter commented on the concept of placing a premium on a subsidiary's value:

> It takes little imagination to see that this rationale, carried to its logical conclusion, compels the inclusion of a control premium, measured by a hypothetical third-party sale value, in all share valuation cases, not just in situations in which the corporation owns its operating assets through controlled subsidiaries. A corporation's control of directly owned assets is at least as great as it would be if those assets were held through controlled subsidiaries.[74]

Since third-party sale value for an operating company would include an "element of value arising from ... the merger," most Delaware appraisal decisions have explicitly rejected valuations based on acquisition value. The principal exceptions are the *Rapid-American, LeBeau* and *Hintmann* cases that involved subsidiaries of holding companies. Applying control premiums to the value of subsidiaries emphasizes form over substance: as discussed previously, an operating business is not worth more as a subsidiary than as a division.

Commentators reject theory that most market prices include an IMD

Is it appropriate to assume that the market prices of guideline companies always include an IMD? No, it is not. Shares may trade in the market at prices that are higher or lower than the value of the company as a whole. There are clear examples of periods when most companies in certain industries trade at prices that exceed the price that any cash buyer would pay. An obvious and conspicuous example was the "dot.com" euphoria in the late 1990s, when market prices of Internet shares commonly exceeded Financial Control Value and therefore precluded most acquisitions (other than stock-for-stock mergers with similarly priced companies).

Several professors of corporate law have questioned the assumption that most market prices include an IMD. Professor Booth wrote, "[I]t is not necessarily the case that actual market price is always less than fair market price. If it were, then there would be no such thing as a fair market price."[75] Booth commented, "A stock that is permanently depressed is presumably just worth less."[76] He observed:

> [A]lthough it is always appropriate to ask whether there is some reason to distrust the market price in any given case, it is clear that the market price is not *always* low [*emphasis in original*]. ... Indeed, in 1999 the *Wall Street Journal* reported several takeovers at negative premiums. Apparently, in the case of these companies the market had risen to a price in excess of control value.[77]

Professors Hamermesh and Wachter concur that premiums in acquisition transactions are not a rational basis for assuming that market prices necessarily include implied minority discounts:

72 8 Del. Code §262(h).

73 *Agranoff* at *51, footnote 45.

74 Hamermesh and Wachter, "The Short and Puzzling Life," p. 15.

75 Booth, p. 130.

76 *Id.*, p. 150.

77 *Id.*, p. 149.

> [I]t is incorrect to make the logical jump that these premiums [paid in acquisitions] reflect some kind of IMD. The fallacy is obvious and analogous to the "dogs that don't bark" metaphor: there are lots of dogs, and most of the time, most dogs are not barking. Similarly, in any given year, the vast majority of companies are not involved in a change of control transaction.[78]

They point out that generally accepted financial theory is that market prices of liquid securities in informed markets represent going-concern value. They conclude, "There is no evidence that such [market] prices systematically and continuously err on the low side, requiring upward adjustment based on an 'implicit minority discount.'"[79]

Professor Carney as well strongly argued against assuming that market prices of most publicly traded shares include a significant IMD:

> [C]ontrol premiums only occur in transactions involving a transfer of control, where there are thought to be gains from trade, either because of a perception by the purchaser that the transaction offers some opportunity to create new value within the target firm or because the bidder believes that the market value of the target's shares is depressed and it can earn an abnormal return by holding target shares until the market price reflects full value [footnotes omitted]. Even if all values, both present and potential, are valued in the market price for the firm's shares, one would not expect to find a discernible control premium in a widely held firm that is well managed and appears to offer little probability of a transfer of control. Any small probability of a control transaction will already be reflected in the market price, because absent a dominant shareholder, all shareholders expect to have an equal opportunity to share in any such premium, should it appear. Absent an actual transfer of control, control premiums represent probabilities of a control transfer at a premium. Where the probability is close to zero, so is the premium.[80]

78 Hamermesh and Wachter,"The Short and Puzzling Life," p. 33.

79 Id.,p.2

80 Carney and Heimendinger, p. 860.

Eric Nath, a San Francisco–based valuation expert, was the first to question the presumption of an implied minority discount in publicly traded share prices. Nath presented this view in a pioneering 1990 *Business Valuation Review* article in which he argued that market prices generally already reflected control value. He pointed out that the freely traded market prices of a company already had incorporated in them the company's financial control positives or negatives.[81] Nath's theory stimulated a great deal of debate and reconceptualization and, despite much initial resistance in publications and seminars, has become widely accepted by leading valuation experts. Mark Lee, an experienced and well-respected valuation expert, pointed out in 2001:

> If there is no M&A market available to sell a company at a premium to its stock market value, then there is little or no acquisition premium, much less a "theoretical" premium based on an average of acquisitions of dissimilar companies.[82]

Lee also pointed out in 2004 that "the acquisition value of a company may be equal to or below its market value," explaining, "While a company may be viewed as very attractive to a purchaser of a minority interest in the public market, the company as a whole may be perceived as too risky at its publicly traded market price."[83] In a recent book about fairness opinions, Philip Clements and Philip Wisler took the same position, stating, "The control value of a company may not differ greatly [from] and may even be below its publicly traded minority share value."[84]

The Court relied upon authors who no longer support IMD

Although the Court of Chancery is becoming aware that the IMD assumption is being questioned, many of their

81 Nath, "Control Premiums and Minority Interest Discounts in Private Companies," *Business Valuation Review*, June 1990. He reiterated this position in "The Tale of Two Markets," *Business Valuation Review*, September 1994, and in "How Public Guideline Companies Represent 'Control' Value for a Private Company," *Business Valuation Review*, December 1997.

82 M. Mark Lee, "Control Premiums and Minority Discounts: the Need for Economic Analysis," *Business Valuation Update*, August 2001, 4.

83 M. Mark Lee, "The Discount for Lack of Control and the Ownership Control Premium," in *The Handbook of Business Valuation and Intellectual Property Analysis*, Robert F. Reilly and Robert P. Schweihs, eds. (New York: McGraw-Hill, 2004), 37.

84 Philip J. Clements and Philip W. Wisler, *The Standard & Poor's Guide to Fairness Opinions*. (New York: McGraw-Hill, 2005), 94.

recent IMD decisions continued to rely on experts' now-abandoned or modified theories. In 2007, Vice Chancellor Lamb noted that there is a debate about IMD, citing the Hamermesh & Wachter and Booth articles which both "argu[e] that the implicit minority discount has not gained general acceptance in the financial community."[85]

In 1996, when Shannon Pratt wrote that the guideline company method "usually requires some adjustment from the publicly traded minority stock value equivalent to account for control," that was the accepted view of the financial community.[86] At that time, the Delaware Court rightly relied upon the financial community's accepted view of an implied minority discount since they were following Weinberger's injunction to make their valuations in accordance with accepted financial theory.

Within three years, Pratt had come to modify his view. In a 1999 article he stated, "Valuation analysts who use the guideline public-company valuation method and then automatically tack on a percentage 'control premium' ... had better reconsider their methodology."[87] Pratt included this comment in the Fourth Edition of *Valuing a Business* in 2000, but the Court apparently was not aware of this change. In *Agranoff* (2001), the Court again relied on Pratt's 1996 view as expressed in the 3rd Edition and on Mercer's 1992 book. The Court stated, "The comparable companies analysis generates an equity value that includes an inherent minority trading discount, because the method depends on comparisons to market multiples derived from trading information for minority blocks of the comparable companies.[88]

In 2001, Pratt further clarified his position in *Business Valuation Discounts and Premiums.* After an extensive discussion of various articles and seminars regarding the issue of whether market prices reflect control value, Pratt quoted

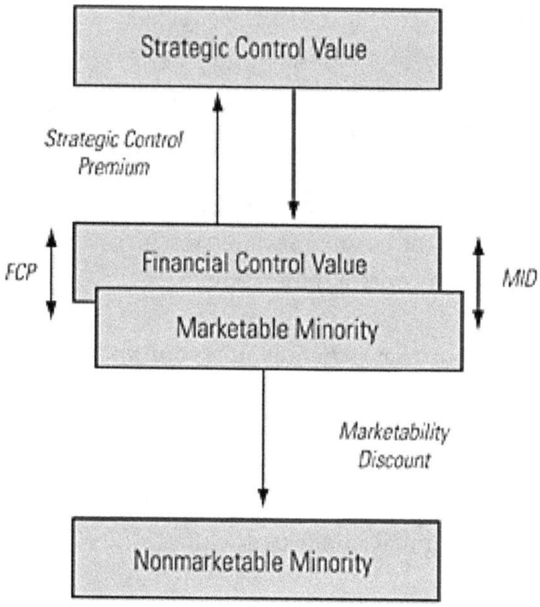

Figure 2: Modified Levels of Value

extensively from Lee's incisive 2001 article and then concluded, "In any case, it is obvious that, given the current state of the debate, one must be extremely cautious about applying a control premium to public market values to determine a control level of value."[89]

However, as late as 2005 in the *Andaloro* decision, the Court continued to cite Pratt's 1996 book in support of an adjustment for IMD.[90] The same Court was clearly aware of Pratt's 4th Edition (2000) because, in the same *Andaloro* decision, it cited the more recent 4th Edition in its discounted cash flow discussion.[91] It is unclear why the Court did not use Pratt's modified view of an implied minority discount in his more recent 4th Edition.

Mercer was also coming to the conclusion that market prices are often close to control value. He addressed the issue directly in 2004 in the important 1st Edition of *The Integrated Theory*

85 *Highfields Capital* at *67, footnote 72.

86 Pratt, Reilly, and Schweihs, *Valuing a Business.* 3rd ed., p. 210.

87 Pratt, "Control Premiums? Maybe, Maybe Not—34% of 3rd Quarter Buyouts at Discounts," *Business Valuation Update,* January 1999, pp. 1–2. This article is cited in Pratt, Reilly and Schweihs. *Valuing a Business: The Analysis and Appraisal of Closely Held Companies.* 4th ed. (New York: McGraw-Hill 2000), 357.

88 *Agranoff* at 892. The footnote to this sentence cites *Le Beau* at *25 and includes the references to the Pratt and Mercer books. (See footnotes 36 and 37 herein.)

89 Pratt, *Business Valuation Discounts and Premiums* (2001), 40.

90 *Andaloro* at *65. See the discussion of this case in Matthews, "A Review of Valuations in Delaware Appraisal Cases, 2004–2005," *Business Valuation Review,* Summer 2006, 59–60, comparing the discussion of control premiums in the 3rd and 4th Editions of Valuing a Business. Hamermesh and Wachter compare those two editions in "The Short and Puzzling Life" on pp. 51–53.

91 *Id.* at *36.

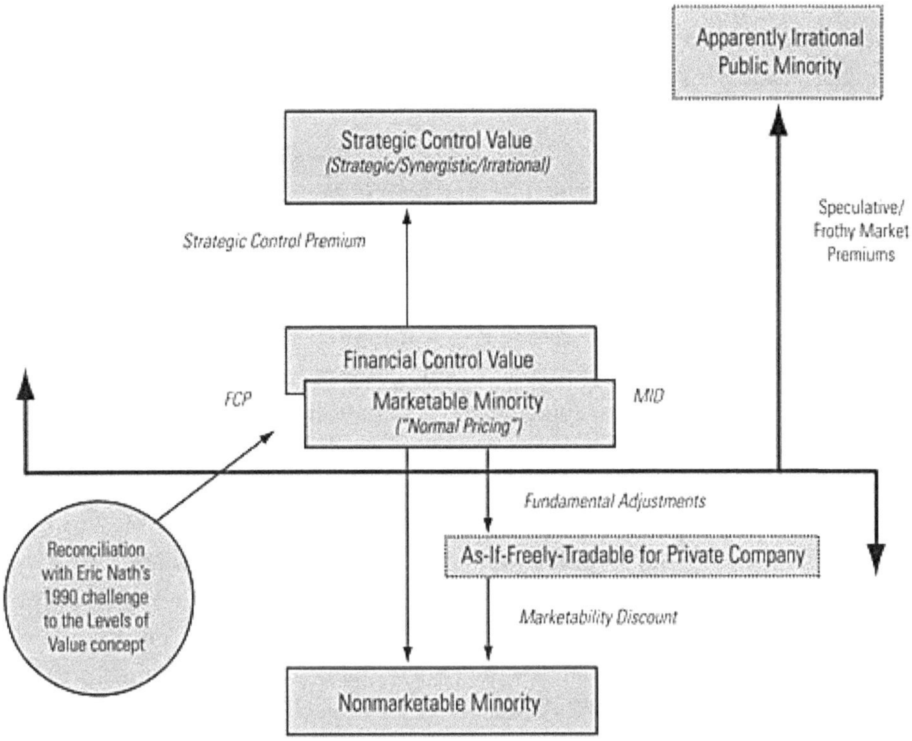

Figure 3: Levels of Value Reconciled with Nath

of Business Valuation.[92] After having disagreed with Nath in the early 1990s, he conceded that Nath had been right, and that the financial control premium (the difference between Financial Control Value and Marketable Minority Value) could be zero.[93] Mercer's 2004 book included a modified levels-of-value diagram (see Figure 2) that showed Marketable Minority Value overlapping Financial Control Value.[94] He uses that model to make the point that "unless there are cash flow-driven differences between the enterprise's financial control value and its marketable minority value, there will be no (or very little) minority interest discount."[95]

Mercer presented an elaborated diagram (see Figure 3) reconciling his levels of value with Nath.[96] This diagram also shows that public market prices may exceed Strategic Control Value at a level he calls "Apparently Irrational" (as in the "dot.com" phenomenon in the late 1990s).

Thus, although citations from Pratt and Mercer supported pre-1999 decisions regarding IMD, since 1999 neither of these prominent authors has supported the concept that publicly traded shares customarily include implied minority discounts.

Testing for IMD

It is not the writer's position that it is never appropriate to adjust for IMD. In fact, the valuator should determine empirically if IMDs exist in the guideline companies' prices. Only if it can be demonstrated that the prices of guideline companies include IMDs is it appropriate to add a control premium to offset those IMDs. Analysis is required to quantify the adjustment. IMD is fact-specific in each valuation and it cannot be determined by using a generic rule of thumb.[97] Nath wrote in 1990:

92 Mercer, *The Integrated Theory of Business Valuation* (Baltimore: Peabody, 2004). This book innovatively showed the interrelation among various approaches to valuation, discounts, and premiums.

93 *Id.*, p. 101.

94 *Id.*, p. 110. This diagram is reproduced in Pratt, *Valuing a Business*, 5th ed. (2008), 387.

95 *Id.*, p. 108.

96 *Id.*, p. 376.

97 The U.S. Tax Court now requires case-specific analyses and rejects generic discounts for lack of marketability. See, *Bernard Mandelbaum v. Commissioner*, T.C. Memo 1995–255 (1995); Pratt, *Valuing a Business*, 5th ed. (2008), 449; Michael A. Paschall, "The 35% 'Standard' Marketability Discount: R.I.P." CCH *Business Valuation Alert* (February 2005), 3.

> It would seem that an appraiser could utilize a control premium only if it could be convincingly demonstrated that the comparative stocks being utilized are undervalued, and a reasonable estimate of the magnitude of undervaluation can be established for each stock, individually. This will be theoretically impossible in an efficient market.[98]

Since the market is sometimes not efficient, IMDs may arise. In examining whether IMDs are present, the key factor to be considered is the relation between market multiples and transaction multiples. It is possible to estimate IMD (if any) by comparing the average multiples of guideline companies with average multiples of guideline transactions. The valuator (and ultimately the Court) should then consider what adjustment should be made to multiples of guideline transactions to eliminate the synergistic benefits that should be excluded in a Delaware appraisal. To the extent that any of the guideline transactions were priced at earlier dates under different market conditions, further adjustments should be considered. IMD can be quantified by reference to the difference between guideline transaction multiples (adjusted for synergy and market conditions) and market multiples of guideline companies. It should also be recognized that prices paid in acquisitions may include the benefits of cost savings that would be excluded under Delaware's "operative reality" concept.

In the author's experience, it is not uncommon for multiples of guideline transactions to be similar to multiples of guideline companies.[99] If the differences between multiples of guideline companies and multiples of guideline transactions (excluding synergies and other adjustments) are not significant, then there is no basis for concluding that IMD is relevant to the valuation. Moreover, if there is an absence of recent guideline transactions, this fact is evidence that market prices of guideline companies are not at levels that are attractive to acquirors and that they therefore have no IMD.[100]

98 Nath, "Control Premiums and Minority Interest Discounts in Private Companies," 45.

99 See Matthews, "Fairness Opinions: Common Errors and Omissions" in *The Handbook of Business Valuation and Intellectual Property Analysis,* Eds. Reilly and Schweihs. (New York: McGraw-Hill, 2004). 215, Exhibit 8–2.

100 The airline industry is an example of a sector in which no cash acquisitions have been made for many years.

Average premiums paid in acquisitions are statistically biased

Testifying experts commonly rely on average premiums paid in transactions as a basis for estimating IMD and as a measure of acquisition premiums. Regrettably, there is a widespread failure to recognize that the data used in calculating the average premiums in transactions includes a substantial built-in upward bias. Because these premiums are computed in relation to the market prices of target companies prior to the announcement of acquisitions, the databases consist primarily of those companies that acquirors believe to be worth more than they are trading for in the market. Thus the universe of guideline transactions includes companies which were *undervalued* in the market but necessarily excludes companies that acquirors consider *overvalued.* Thousands of companies are publicly traded, but only a small portion of them are acquired in any specific year. Professor Bradford Cornell took the position fifteen years ago, that most market prices do not include an IMD, saying, "The fact that most **companies do not receive takeover bids** at premiums above market price indicates investors believe that the shares of those companies are not worth significantly more than market price" [*emphasis in original*].[101] Pratt wrote in 2001:

> Out of the tens of thousands of public companies only a small percentage actually are acquired each year. In recent years the companies purchased have often been "best of breed," making them a very unique subset of the market. Statistically, it is unlikely that this small, select group is universally representative of the market as a whole.[102]

The Chancery Court's belief that guideline companies suffer from IMD, and the Court's quantifications of those IMDs, have generally been based on expert testimony as to the average premiums paid in acquisitions. The Court, therefore, has relied on data that is seriously flawed and statistically unreliable.

101 Bradford Cornell, Corporate Valuation (New York: McGraw-Hill, 1993), 243.

102 Pratt. 2001. Business Valuation Discounts and Premiums, 60.

The Courts have been further misled by the fact that some investment bankers erroneously include average premiums as one of several measures in arriving at fairness opinions. Even though the use of average premiums is not statistically valid, the use of average acquisition premiums has been mistakenly accepted by many in the financial community. The investment bankers' analyses are available in proxy statements for mergers and acquisitions, giving the reliance on average premiums a façade of respectability. The author has criticized the use of average acquisition premiums as a fairness standard in several publications over the past two decades, as have Eric Nath, Shannon Pratt and Mark Lee.[103]

Conclusion

- It is clear that leading legal and valuation commentators have concluded that there is no basis for assuming that market prices of all publicly traded shares include an implicit minority discount. The default assumption should be that publicly traded shares sell at a company's going-concern value. If petitioner's expert concludes that an IMD is appropriate in a given situation, its magnitude should be based on a comparison between acquisition multiples and market multiples.

- The concept that a subsidiary of a company should be valued with an acquisition premium, even though an operating company is valued without such a premium, is illogical: it elevates form over substance. There is no support in the valuation or finance literature for this distinction. A business is not worth more if it is a subsidiary rather than a division of an operating business. Valuation experts should apply any relevant premiums without distinction as to the legal form of the business unless the distinction leads to a difference in cash flows.

- Average acquisition premiums paid for shares of publicly traded companies are statistically biased and therefore are a misleading measure of control premiums in valuations.

***Gilbert E. Matthews**, CFA, is Senior Managing Director and Chairman of Sutter Securities Incorporated in San Francisco, California.* *The writer gratefully acknowledges the contribution of Dr. Michelle Patterson and numerous others who offered helpful comments.*

103 See, e.g., Matthews and Lee, "Fairness Opinions & Common Stock Valuations," in *The Library of Investment Banking,* Vol. IV. Ed. Robert Kuhn, (New York: Dow Jones Irwin, 1990), 407; Nath, "Control Premiums and Minority Interest Discounts in Private Companies," 41–43; Lee and Matthews, "Fairness Opinions," in *The Handbook of Advanced Business Valuation.* Eds. Reilly and Schweihs (New York: McGraw-Hill, 2000), 327; Matthews, "Fairness Opinions," In *Business Valuations for the Legal Practitioner* (Chicago: American Bar Association Center for Continuing Legal Education, 2001), K14–15; Lee, "Control Premiums and Minority Discounts: the Need for Economic Analysis," 2–4; Lee, "The Discount for Lack of Control and the Ownership Control Premium" and Matthews, "Fairness Opinions: Common Errors and Omissions," in *The Handbook of Business Valuation and Intellectual Property Analysis.* 43 and 214–216; Pratt, *Valuing a Business,* 5th ed. (2008), 391–392 (quoting the writer).

Implied Minority Discount in Statutory Fair Value: The Doctrine that Just Won't Die

If your fair value appraisal shows up in the Delaware Chancery Court, it might be best to start by recalling a famous line from the movie *Cool Hand Luke*: "What we have here is a failure to communicate." That was the major theme of panelists at the recent 2009 ASA Advanced BV Conference in Boston, who spoke on the implied minority discount (IMD) in Delaware and statutory fair value appraisal law.

"There's a gap in communication between folks who make the legal standards regarding fair value and folks like you who actually *do* it," Professor Lawrence Hamermesh (Widener Univ. School of Law) said. The Delaware Chancery Court, in particular—long considered as the "Supreme Court" of business corporation precedent—may have taken a wrong-turn approach when valuing stock in a going concern on behalf of dissenting shareholders.

FV statute leaves a lot to interpretation. A dissenting shareholder action typically takes place after a "squeeze-out" merger by the majority owners. In this context, Delaware law requires courts to appraise the dissenting shares within an "entire fairness/fair price" framework. Specifically, §262(h) of the controlling Delaware statute directs courts to determine the "fair value" of the shares "exclusive of any element of value arising from the accomplishment or expectation of the merger."

Pursuant to this standard, Delaware courts award dissenters a proportional share of the "going concern value"—the present value of anticipated returns assuming the enterprise continued without the merger and the "forced" seller(s) kept their holdings. In a larger sense, the goal is to give dissenters the value of "what's been taken away." The result is (or should be) a Pareto optimum: the dissenters lose nothing and the majority gets the benefit of the proposed merger.

But there's unresolved ambiguity in several of the concepts. For example, Hamermesh asks "what's the scope of the exclusion and what is 'fair?'" And what about the values that could arise from the merger—how do you protect dissenting shareholders from an opportunistic majority that wants to squeeze them out prior to a potentially profitable combination?

In addition, application of the going concern standard raises two issues: 1) marketability and other discounts generally do not apply, and 2) hypothetical or actual third-party sale values (observable market prices) aren't controlling. "The cases strongly suggest that even established synergies are not supposed to be considered in a stand-alone, going concern valuation of an entity," Hamermesh confirms.

The Delaware courts prefer the discounted cash flow (DCF) method when implementing a going concern value because it's based on the anticipated cash flow returns from the company as it is currently organized—including the pluses and minuses of current management, operations, and customers—including all the "warts and diamonds," as Hamermesh put it. Further, when the DCF uses an exit multiple, the courts will not adjust the terminal value and they have declined to increase the ultimate value (by lowering the cost of equity) despite dissenters' arguments that the DCFs reflect the cost of equity in the form of minority holdings.

"The DCF gives courts all they want, they think," Hamermesh said, "and then all they have to do is determine the dissenters' appropriate share."

What is the controversy? When reliable DCF data are not available, the Delaware courts will consider a guideline public company or comparable company analysis (CCA)—essentially applying public shareholder market multiples to the going concern value of the subject. Finance theory generally holds that shares of public companies, whether of the comparables or the subject, trade at enterprise value divided by the number of outstanding shares. Thus, to move from share value to enterprise value is an exercise in simple multiplication. "No finance text holds that the result has to be adjusted upward on the premise that the comparable companies' share prices impound some inappropriate discount," Hamermesh said.

Delaware courts have had problems reaching the same conclusion. The judicial view starts with the premise that enterprises are "routinely sold" at a premium relative to their trading price. Second, synergies account for only some—and perhaps very little—of such acquisition premiums. Thus, the enterprise value necessarily exceeds its trading value, essentially because courts view the shares and the entity as separate commodities: The shares have limited rights and—in particular—limited control, and do not reflect the full enterprise value. To disperse the element of control over all shares, the courts adjust the CCA upward, based on this implied minority discount (IMD), which derived from observed acquisition premiums in the comparable data. As the Delaware Chancery Court explained 10 years ago:

> [CCA analysis] produces an equity valuation that inherently reflects a minority discount, as the data used for [the] comparison is all derived from minority trading of comparable companies. Because *that value is not fully reflective of the intrinsic worth of the corporation on a going concern basis,* this court has applied an explicit control premium in calculating the fair value of the equity in an appraisal proceeding. *Borruso v. Communications Telesystems Int'l.,* 753 A.2d 451,458 (Del. Ch. 1999)(emphasis added)

According to Hamermesh, this premium can be substantial, with the more recent cases favoring "adjustments" up to 30%.

How Pratt may have planted the IMD 'weed.' The IMD first appeared in cases in 1992 and 1995 but didn't become entrenched until *LeBeau v. M.G. Bancorporation* (1998 Del. Ch. LEXIS 9), when the majority shareholders hired Shannon Pratt. In arguing for the application of the IMD, the dissenters pointed to an excerpt from Pratt's *Valuing a Buisness* (3rd ed.1996), which stated that the guideline public company analysis usually requires some adjustment to account for control.

That was the generally accepted view at the time—with only a few early detractors (in particular, Eric Nath and Mark Lee) who argued that the prices of freely traded companies already included dispersed control. By 2000, Pratt changed his mind. "Valuation analysts who use [CCA] and then automatically tack on a percentage 'control premium'...had better reconsider their methodology," he wrote in the 4th edition of his familiar text. Chris Mercer also updated his position in *Business Valuation: An Integrated Theory*. As a result, the predominant view among BV professionals came to reject the implied discount in minority share pricing.

In 2001 however, in *Agronoff v. Miller* (791 A.2d 880), the Delaware Chancery Court cited Pratt's 1996 and Mercer's 1992 editions, despite the availability of the updated versions that discredited the IMD doctrine. Given the weight of precedent in judicial opinions and the resistance to overturning prior law, the court has stuck to the doctrine and cited these older authorities as support, even in cases as recent as 2003 and 2004. Gil Matthews, who also spoke to the ASA audience, acknowledged the irony that "neither Pratt nor Mercer currently support the position that the courts keep citing them for!"

"It makes you wonder whether the formal litigation process is the best way for sound, rational analysis to come out," Hamermesh said. The IMD now seems mandatory—an entrenched "doctrinal weed" among Delaware statutory appraisal law.

Disputing the IMD. After more than a decade of IMD cases, Hamermesh and his frequent co-author Michael Wachter (Univ. of Penn.) can't find any rational or financial basis for the doctrine. "The IMD doesn't make sense," Hamermesh said. "How can it be squared with contemporary corporate finance theory that says efficient market prices reflect the pro rata value of the firm's free cash flows?"

Hamermesh's argument is twofold. First, when a company issues public shares, it creates agency costs (i.e., separation of ownership from control, including the costs of monitoring management, decreasing direct performance incentives, etc.). Pubic traders price those additional costs going into the investment as part of the company's "operative reality." (Such additional costs are "one of the warts," Hamermesh told the ASA audience.) Thus the fair value of public shares cannot exclude the impact of such costs.

Second, to whom does control value truly belong? "If agency costs are not eliminated until a going private transaction (just like synergies), then including the value of control contradicts the controlling Delaware statute," Hamermesh states. How do you justify paying dissenters the value of control when they already belong to the larger shareholder class to which control has been dispersed through the public offering? Put another way, "If shareholders were truly entitled to getting the value of control in a statutory fair value appraisal, then shouldn't the DCF values be adjusted upward to account for reduced agency costs?"

Instead, courts only adjust the CCA results upward. "The IMD posits that, no matter how liquid and informed the financial markets, all publicly traded shares trade in the market at a substantial discount relative to the going concern value using a DCF," Hamermesh said. "The IMD amounts to a statement that financial markets consistently price shares significantly below pro rata going concern value."

What to do going forward. "Cite the current positions," Matthews suggested, "and point out the fallacies of courts continuing to apply the IMD." Hamermesh added that to pull the precedential weed, appraisers must be willing to state publicly—though not necessarily in litigation—that this rationale doesn't work. To the courts, Hamermesh and co-author Wachter suggest creating a safeguard against majority "opportunism" by:

- Accepting evidence of post-merger business development (as in *Del. Open MRI Radiology Assoc. v. Kessler*, 898 A.2d 290 (Del. Ch. 2006);

- Adjusting projected cash flows upward, on a case-by-case basis (possibly using hindsight or "book of wisdom" data);

- Recognizing that breach of fiduciary duty cases remain an alternative option and protection for dissenters; and

- Adopting a penalty default (using the IMD methodology) when the "squeezing" majority fails to present a meaningful or reliable DCF.

While the IMD may not make economic sense, it may apply when the court is suspicious of the majority's motives and/or the majority is not cooperating by providing reliable projections. "Courts may not be good at doing valuations," Hamermesh said, "but they are good at looking at the structure of deals and investigating the limits of the majority imposing their will on the minority."

Judicial decision-making should continue to focus on its strengths—protecting the rights and interests of those who might otherwise be trampled—while appraisers should focus on their strengths. "We're all working toward a convergence of thought and shared conceptualization of fair value appraisals," Matthews said. A good sign: In a poll of the ASA audience, at least half raised their hands when asked if they'd used an implied minority discount in the past, but only a couple of stalwarts kept their hands in the air when asked if they'd continue to do so in the future.

For additional reading: Take a look at the article by Hamermesh and Wachter, "Rationalizing Appraisal Standards in Compulsory Buy-outs," available at http://papers.ssrn.com/sol3/papers.cfm?abstract_id=1244665. Also good: Gil Matthews' recent piece, "Misuse of Control Premiums in Delaware Appraisals," 27 *Business Valuation Review* (2008). Matthews highly recommended the latest edition of *Business Valuation Integrated Theory*, by Chris Mercer and Travis Harms (Wiley Financial, 2008). "It's an excellent tie of financial theory to practice," he said, "and should be on every BV practitioner's bookshelf, along with Pratt."

General Analysis from the Mergerstat®/ BVR Control Premium Study™

The following presents general trend analysis from the *Mergerstat®/BVR Control Premium Study™*, available at BVMarketData.com. The *Mergerstat®/BVR Control Premium Study™* is a premier, online searchable database that generates empirical support for quantifying control premiums, implied minority discounts, and public company valuation multiples. The database is updated quarterly and a subscription to the database includes unlimited searches for a full year, as well as the current and historical quarterly control premiums reports—a fully downloadable 70+ page document.

The summary information in this document is only a guide as to what can be done with the *Mergerstat®/BVR Control Premium Study™*. The data in this Analysis should not be used in a valuation report because the summary data is not company specific to a valuation. The appraiser should tailor their search of the database so that the search results match the characteristics of the subject company.

The common thought is that, by using financial transactions to derive a control premium (acquisitions where the

Median Control Premiums
Non-Financial Buyers vs. Financial Buyers

	2000	2001	2002	2003	2004	2005	2006	2007	2008	2009
Non-Financial	28.0%	27.3%	23.7%	35.6%	23.6%	18.9%	20.1%	20.7%	25.5%	40.6%
Financial	34.3%	20.2%	33.0%	33.3%	17.0%	11.7%	15.1%	12.0%	26.0%	24.9%

Source: The Mergerstat®/BVR Control Premium Study™. For more information, visit BVMarketData.com. Research performed on 3/11/2010.

Notes: Non-financial buyers, in this chart, include those buyers making conglomerate acquisitions, horizontal acquisitions, vertical acquisitions, and strategic acquisitions.

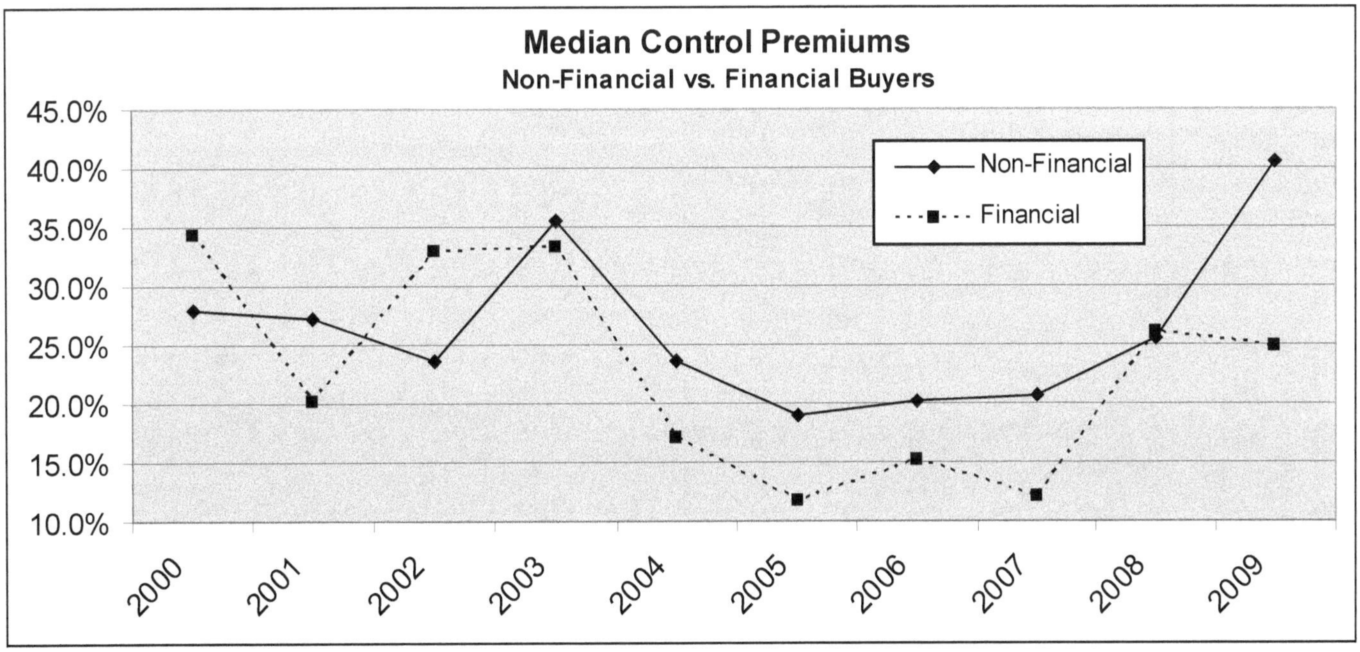

acquirer was a financial buyer), one can help eliminate any synergies that may be present in non-financial buyer acquisitions. This is because financial transactions involve buyers who are primarily looking to make a financial investment in acquiring the company, or have no previous operations. A non-financial buyer—such as a strategic buyer, a horizontal acquisition, a vertical acquisition, or other—may reap synergies from the acquisition.

In other words, the control premium derived from financial acquirer transactions may be more representative of a true control premium; a premium that does not reflect synergies. If this is the case, generally speaking, a comparable non-financial acquisition should have a larger premium than its financial buyer counterpart.

Target Invested Capital (TIC) is calculated as the sum of implied market value of equity plus the face value of total interest bearing debt and the book value of preferred stock outstanding prior to the announcement date. Earnings before interest and taxes (EBIT) and earnings before interest, taxes, depreciation and amortization (EBITDA) are based on the latest reported 12-month period prior to the transaction's announcement date.

Valuation multiples may display trends over time. From this graph, it appears that both the TIC/EBIT and TIC/EBITDA multiples dipped in 2001, before gradually climbing to their peak around 2007. In 2008 and 2009, the multiples seem to be trending downwards.

Median Valuation Multiples

	2000	2001	2002	2003	2004	2005	2006	2007	2008	2009
TIC/EBIT	12.9	10.9	11.0	13.0	14.0	14.4	16.0	16.3	14.1	12.3
TIC/EBITDA	8.9	7.4	7.5	8.5	9.4	9.4	11.2	11.2	10.2	7.7

Source: The Mergerstat®/BVR Control Premium Study™. For more information, visit BVMarketData.com. Research performed on 3/11/2010.

Notes: TIC = Target Invested Capital = Target company's implied total invested capital (TIC) based on the sum of implied market value of equity plus the face value of total interest bearing debt and the book value of preferred stock outstanding prior to the announcement date.

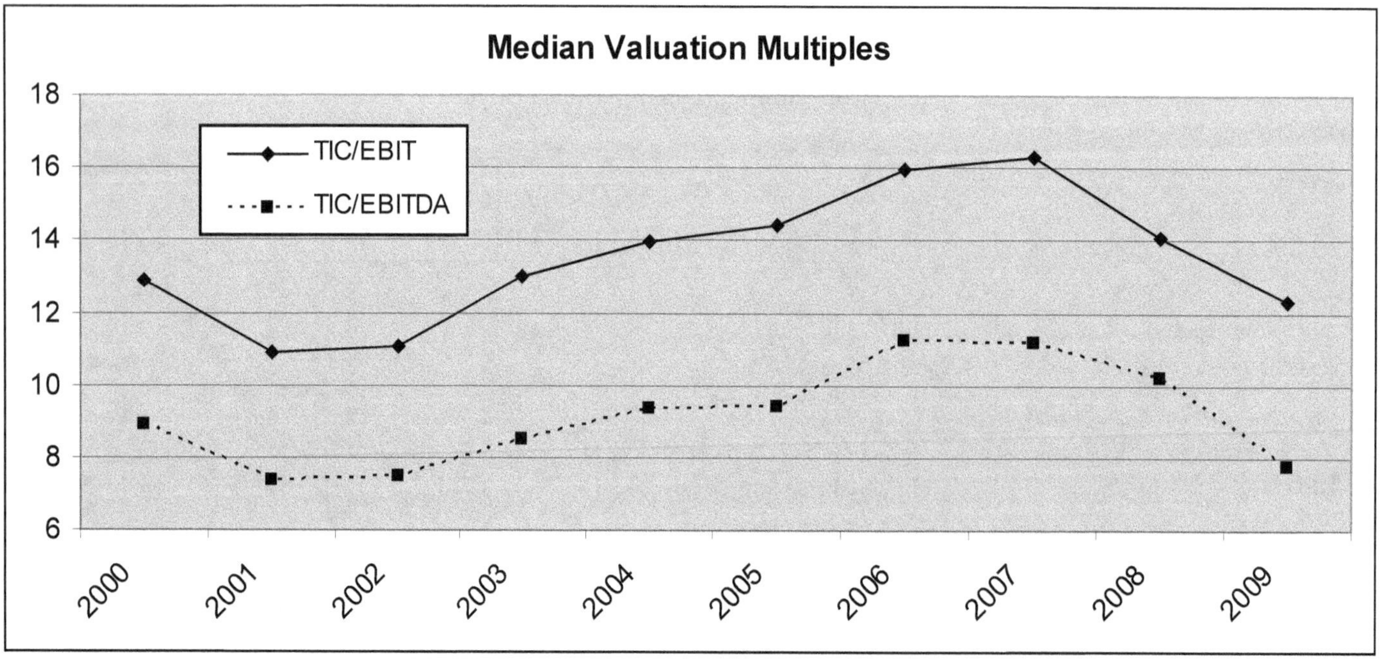

BVR
What It's Worth

Control Premiums: Applications & Analysis

April 29, 2010
Brad Pursel, CPA/ABV, CFA, ASA
Mark J. Edwards, CPA/ABV, CFA
Andrew S. Fargason, CFA

Blake Lyman: Hello, and welcome to "Control Premiums: Applications and Analysis." My name is Blake Lyman, Professional Program Manager of BVR.

Today we draw our attention to control premiums, whose day in the sun is quickly coming, if not already here. With increased scrutiny from a number of bodies, the use and application of control premiums is requiring more appraiser justification and documentation than ever, while still requiring the same amount of appraiser judgment. Joining us today to discuss these and other issues are Brad Pursel, Mark Edwards, and Andrew Fargason.

Brad Pursel is a principle with Brown Smith Wallace, LLC in Saint Louis, Missouri. He specializes in the valuation of business, intangible assets, and intellectual property for financial and tax reporting, transaction planning, and litigation support purposes. In addition, Brad provides calculations of damages and serves as an expert witness in litigation matters.

Mark Edwards is partner in evaluation services practice at Grant Thornton, LLC, and serves as the practice leader for the southeastern region. Prior to joining Grant Thornton, Mark spent over 13 working with a Big Five public accounting firm, and other national valuation firms. Mark has been working in valuation profession for more than 20 years, and has worked with numerous public and private clients on financial reporting, litigation, transaction advisory, and strategic planning.

Andrew S. Fargason is the managing director of the Atlanta Financial Evaluation Group of American Appraisal. He has completed business enterprise and capital stock valuations for mergers and acquisitions, financial reporting, estate planning, and gifting purposes. His extensive experience in providing valuation opinions for a variety of intangible assets and derivative securities for US and international GAAP reporting purposes. Andrew is also a member of the Appraisal Foundations Working Group on Control Premiums, Best Practices, and Evaluation for Financial Reporting.

It's my pleasure to welcome Brad, Mark, and Andrew today and you can read much more about them on the web page for today's teleconference.

A few additional announcements: We've made some adjustments to the presentation slides for today's conference. So if you have access to our reading page please feel free to go back and download those again, or pull them from the conference materials section on our BeaconLive Web platform.

Before we begin we'd like to start out with a brief survey on a few issues related to a few issues related to the use of control premiums with our audience.

Question number one: "Do you always apply control premiums to the market capitalization of your public company client under FAS 142/ASC 350 impairment testing?"

Question number two: "If a control premium is applied under the guideline public company method, I typically: either apply the same control premium to all public companies, or vary the control premium by public company?"

Question number three: "If a control premium is applied I typically will support the magnitude of the control premium by cash flow analysis." Please select yes or no.

Here we have question four just coming up on your screen now. "If a control premium is applied, I typically will support the magnitude of the control premium by analyzing the implied market multiples." Here again the options are yes and no.

And finally question number five. "If a control premium is applied, I typically apply a control premium to the company's equity or invested capital."

While we wait for those results to be tabulated, I'd like to switch over now to the presentation portion of our teleconference. And with that we welcome in Brad Pursel. Brad, I will turn it over to you. Take it away.

Brad Pursel: Okay. Super. Thanks, Blake.

Before we begin the presentation getting into too much detail, I wanted to go over a little bit of, I guess, set the stage for our discussion. Certainly there's theoretical debate, and some analysts have argued that control premium should rarely be used if ever. For much of our discussion today, we will assume that control premium, but theoretically the application for control premium we've decided that it would be acceptable.

Certainly we have no intention of providing any sort of rule of thumb in terms of a control premium. There's really no short cut to performing a thorough valuation analysis of your subject entity, which would likely focus on expected cash flows and required rates of return. Control premium data may be included in your valuation analysis, but we don't believe that that citing control premium studies should be a substitute for a more rigorous valuation analysis.

In addition, many of our examples today with – our discussion will focus on financial reporting applications, most particularly as it relates to goodwill impairment testing. However, we believe that much of what's going to be discussed today would be appropriate for other valuation purposes as well. In terms of discussing the applications of control premium data, we're going to focus on either adjusting public company clients market cap upwards or adjusting guideline public company market cap upwards for some sort of guideline company method.

Today, we will not specifically be addressing the use of control premium data to calculate implied minority interest discounts. In addition, many of our examples will be focused on acquisitions of 100 percent or significant controlling interest entities. So for instance, we're not going to get into issues related to, say, the valuation of a 50 percent interest in an entity. That's not really what we're going to be covering today.

For my prepared remarks today, I'm going to focus on an overview of control premium issues and also discuss some specifics about control premium data. Starting out here we have some basic discussions of control premium in terms of what do we mean by control premium and what is meant by control. And I've laid out here the definitions that are provided in the *International Glossary of Business Valuation Terms.* And one thing that's clear: when you do any sort of research of the literature that are in control premiums is that what's meant by the term "control premium" is not always clear.

As defined here, I would argue that as defined on this slide "control premium" is really focused on some sort of idea of financial control and not really strategic control. In other words, it's focused on the ability of management to increase cash flows or lower risk for the subject company by changing strategies and how the businesses manage. It doesn't really address something that's better described as strategic control, which is a premium that depends upon combination of another entity to generate a higher value. And so I think some of the debate around control premium involves what is actually meant by the term "control premium."

So today I will try to specify strategic control premium and financial control premium when appropriate, when I'm just generically describing control premium. It's something that may reflect either type of control, or it may just reflect the fact that we're just looking at some sort of acquisition premium that was above the publicly traded stock price.

This becomes important. It's not strictly just hair-splitting. It becomes very important, because when you're defining your valuation engagement it's important to consider whether the standard value is such that it would be appropriate to consider, let's say, that the hypothetical buyer may be a strategic buyer who would factor synergies into the purchase price.

Although some may argue the synergies are inconsistent with the fair market value standard, certainly including synergies under FASB's fair value standard may be appropriate if it is determined that market participants would include strategic buyers. And this also brings up the concept of level of value. Arguably there are two different levels of value that we're kind of dealing with here. One is strategic control and the other is financial control.

It's important to understand what your objective is in terms of when you're performing valuation, and it's also important to understand whether the level of value underlying your market transactions, whether it be control premium data or looking at transaction multiples. It's important to understand whether those value indications were strategic control or financial control.

I would certainly refer the listeners to a book written by Chris Mercer and Travis Harms titled, *Integrated Theory of Business Valuation.* They go and do some of these concepts in a lot more detail than we can today. So as described it's important to distinguish between financial and strategic control because the possibility exists that you believe that the appropriate level of value is financial control, and yet your indications of value are all strategic control. It's really an issue of making sure that you're making an apples-to-apples comparison in very simple terms, because this might have a bearing on not only the sort of market data that you're looking at, but also the sort of cash flow adjustments that you may be using in your valuation.

Another thing to consider in terms of control premiums is the fact that this data, there is an inherent bias in the control premium data in that the transactions completed arguably have reflected target companies that have been determined to be good acquisition targets. So the main point is this: simply because other public companies have been acquired at a premium to their market cap does not mean that buyers exist who are willing to pay a premium to acquire any public company. Certainly this sort of bias has been discussed in articles by the likes of, say, Eric Nath and Gill Mathews, and I think also Mark Lee, among others.

In terms of methods used to measure control – and it could be strategic or financial – there's really three basic methods I would say that we see in practice. The first would be quantifying the cash flows; actually trying to bake any sort of control type adjustment into your cash flow stream.

The second would be by applying transaction multiples that potentially reflect the existence of some sort of control premium in the multiples themselves. So you're applying those multiples to financial data that hasn't been adjusted.

Then the third method would be simply applying control premium to values, let's say coming from a market cap that arguably could be considered some sort of non-controlling interest value.

Even though number one, the cash flow adjustment, could be straightforward – it could be considered the most straightforward and theoretically most supportable, even this method could be problematic.

Let's take a simple example: If you're valuing Acme Public Company and your analysis indicates that it's appropriate to determine a level of strategic control value – if you're taking Acme Public Company's market cap and adding your estimate of synergies to its market cap, there are two potential challenges. One, well, you need to estimate the portion of the synergy value that whatever is actually shared with Acme Public Company in an acquisition scenario. And then two, if the market already recognizes that Acme Public Company is a potential takeover target then theoretically the market cap may already include a premium related to the likelihood that Acme Public Company would be acquired by, let's say, a strategic buyer. This concept is described in detail in one of the readings we suggested for this teleconference, "The Value of Control" white paper written by Damodaran.

The third method, applying the control premium – what I think we'll show here in our discussion of this issue is that there are so many potential factors that could influence an observed control premium that it may be unlikely that a one size fits all control premium could be applied to a public company. That would be whether you're valuing a public company client for purposes of impairment testing or whether you're valuing various public companies under the guideline company method, and using that to determine the value of your subject company. The information that I've looked at leads me to believe that really you need to do that sort of discreet analysis on a company-by-company basis before applying a control premium.

There are some basic assumptions that are being made by an analyst who is applying a control premium. Clearly, before you apply a control premium as mentioned before, you obviously need to make sure that you understand the appropriate standard value and level of value desired. In other words, are you trying to obtain a financial control or a strategic control level of value? Because that may impact the sort of analysis that you do and the sort of transactions that you include in your analysis.

The basic assumptions, I would say, are one, that the public company's share price understates the value of 100 percent equity due to one of more of the following: prices could be on a minority interest basis; the current share price is not accurately measured by the fair value of a minority interest; the nature of the public company is such that there could be synergies that could be generated by another buyer.

The second basic assumption is that there is an assumption that the valuation specialist can actually quantify a reasonable premium to apply to the public company's share price or to the public company cash flows. This determination may be based upon a number of items: looking at the subject company's trading history; guideline company multiples; historical transaction multiples; certainly, forecasted company cash flows, which may include strategic adjustments or other control adjustments; and obviously looking at historical control premium data.

Then the third fundamental assumption would be that there are actually potential buyers or market participants that exist in the market willing to pay a premium to acquire the public company. So in considering the third item, one of the things that analysts may want to look at recent M&A activity in the subject company's industry. In addition, there may be industry research, which indicates that analysts and other industry experts are expecting that M&A activity will be on the rise in the near term.

Certainly when working with public company clients it is not unusual for management to indicate that their stock is undervalued; and this particularly occurred quite often during the fourth quarter of 2008 and the first quarter of 2009. If that is something that's being considered in terms of your discussions with management and their beliefs on how their stock price, whether or not it represents fair value.

I do think it is helpful to understand and potentially document factors that may support a belief by management that the stock price does not actually reflect fair value or intrinsic value. But certainly I wouldn't say that any of these items are necessarily indicative that the stock is under priced. So some of the factors that I've looked at in the past would certainly be high stock price volatility, such as existed during the fourth quarter and first quarter of a year ago, low float for the stock, low trading volume, lack of analyst coverage, and the presence of asymmetric information.

With the first four items, those are data points that an analyst could find for any company including your guideline public companies. In terms of asymmetric information, that's really only information that most likely an analyst would come up with if you're actually working with a public company client. Let's say they've got a new product or service launch or new customer win or new market entrance, something that the investing public does not yet know about but they do. Those are actually factors that reasonably could expect the market's expectations of cash flows for this business to differ from those of management. So those are again some of the items that we look at in making that determination.

Continuing along those lines, some other factors that we'll look at as described here, bullish indicators: positive analyst recommendations. Obviously you need to be weary of potential for analyst bias, stock redemptions, insider purchases, debt capital issuances. Obviously these items are not determinative of whether or not it's appropriate to apply a control premium. But I do think in documenting the application of control premium and why it's done, these might be items to include in your work papers that certainly if management is arguing that they think their stock is underpriced these sort of actions at least would be arguably consistent with that belief. On the flip side, bearish indicators include negative analyst recommendations, stock issuances, insider sales, and then also short interest levels.

Obviously it's unlikely that management would indicate that they're stock is underpriced that it's unlikely that if you're working with a public company client, they're going to say, "Hey, yeah, we actually mismanaged the company's assets, and we're not optimizing the value of the company." So it's unlikely you're going to ever have that sort of conversation.

But one potential factor to consider when you're assessing the company's stock price and whether or it's priced appropriately is that to take a look at corporate governance ratings for public company. Poor corporate governance ratings would theoretically increase the possibility that a public company is not being optimally managed, and therefore potentially there would be a need to consider a financial control adjustment to value. There's a pretty good discussion of this concept in Damodoran's paper, "The Value of Control," which I've mentioned previously.

Okay. Now we are ready to start digging to some of the specifics related to control premium data. I'm sure everyone is familiar with the basic calculation of a control premium. It's important to mention that Mergerstat and other sources often calculate these premiums over various periods of time preceding the announcement. It could be one day, one week, one month, and two months. Mergerstat also calculates what it calls a Mergerstat control premium, which is based upon what they describe as the unaffected price, which they determine based upon analysis of trading volume and information that may indicate whether a company was subject to takeover rumors prior to the announcement date.

Theoretically if you use the Mergerstat control premium that would remove any affects of information leakage regarding the transaction and lead to a more accurate measurement of the premium. In terms of the data sources, I've listed two here. Historically I've used the Mergerstat Review Book and the Mergerstat®/BVR Control Premium Study™. What I've kind of found over time is that I like using the database more. I think it's a good tool as it permits a more targeted search for appropriate transactions depending upon the specific needs of your valuation engagement. Another source that I wanted to mention would be fairness options that are typically included within proxy filings for public companies prior to shareholder approval of an acquisition.

Most of these proxy filings, which are referred to as Schedule 14(a) filings have a fairly comprehensive discussion that typically will include a discussion of control premiums observed from relevant transactions. So that is yet another source again. Those are the filings with the SEC. I think whatever source you use the goal is pretty straightforward. You want to spend less time actually searching for transactions and more time actually doing a thorough analysis of the seller companies underlying the control premium data. More importantly your subject company's cash flow discount rate, and other relevant market data.

So in terms of the control premium data, one question that I think is appropriate to raise is, well, does the data that we're generically calling control premium data, does the observed premium data actually reflect control? I think there's certainly many reasons why that could not be the case. Going down the line here, one, we've got that the value paid reflects changing suboptimal management policy. So that's arguably financial control, not strategic control. Two, you could have market participant level synergies. That's a strategic control level of value. You could have buyer specific synergies. Well, that's – depending upon your definition of value, you may say that shouldn't be factored in to financial control or strategic control value.

Number four, you have an asset that was simply undervalued by the market. Number five, which was just added recently, we've got market returns between measurement date and acquisition date, which I'll go into more detail about. Number six, the asset value already includes a value attributable to an acquisition via information leakage or investor expectations regarding and acquisition. Number seven, stupidity or management hubris. Number eight, negotiation skill. And number nine, psychological factors, which I'll talk about in more detail later on.

In addition, per Damodaran, he also discussed some non-control factors in a BVR teleconference from about four years ago, so he covered information leakage, motives of buyers, i.e. synergies, undervalued stock, which I've talked about, and also management hubris or the stupidity premium.

So again, when you're starting your assignment and you need to know the appropriate level of value that you're trying to achieve, right? That's a fundamental objective at the start of engagement. Then obviously when you then dig into something such as control premium data, you need to try to understand as much as you can. Well, what does this premium data what does it really measure? What can I glean from that data if I'm not really sure why the premium was paid. So in terms of number four, which as Damodaran would describe it, it would just be all the stock prices is wrong or the stock is underpriced.

An example of that arguably would be the recent acquisition of Burlington Northern Santa Fe by Berkshire Hathaway. And I'll discuss this though it's not in the slides. Berkshire Hathaway paid $100 per share or about a 32 percent premium on a $75 stock price in a deal that was announced October 2009, and it closed in February 2010. Berkshire Hathaway, as most people, know is run by Warren Buffett, and Berkshire Hathaway is not considered to be a strategic buyer of BNSF. Warren Buffet indicated in a press release that simply that in his belief, it's a $34 billion investment in BNSF. It's a huge bet on the company, the CEO, his team, and the railroad industry. Most important of all, however it's an all in wager on the economic future of the United States. "I love these bets." So that's his quote.

If you look at the proxy filing, the proxy file by BNSF when Buffett approached the CEO regarding the acquisition, and I quote, "Mr. Buffett expressed his belief that the fair value for BNSF's common stock was in the mid-90s per share, and therefore $100 was the highest beat Berkshire Hathaway would be willing to pay." So therefore, based upon Mr. Buffet's belief and fundamental analysis, and belief that markets are not always efficient, the premium paid in this instance largely reflects an instance where the buyer believed that the target's current stock price did not reflect fair value. So arguably, financial control and strategic control have no part of this acquisition, and then further in the proxy the management described how a strategic buyer was not viewed as being the realistic acquirer due to regulatory issues.

Further in the proxy filing, BNSF management cites approval of the offer did include consideration of a 32 percent premium to the closing price on the day prior to the acquisition, and a 36.9 percent premium to the average closing price over the prior 12 month period. In terms of their 52 week high – well, it's actually a 13-month high. The last time BNSF's stock price had been at or above $100 per share was September 2008, which is about 13 months prior to the offer. Certainly the proxy filing details a lot more thorough analysis by the investment bankers in supporting the $100 stock price offer. So that's an example of say the stock being underpriced by the market, and that was what's being imbedded in that premium that's called a control premium.

In terms of the fifth item that I read to you that marketer turns between measurement date and acquisition date might be included. There was a research paper published in 2008 in the *Journal of Business Valuation and Economic Loss Analysis* written by Dan Jordan and Paul Hock, who I believe are associated with Golden Gate University. They pointed out that the unaffected price used to calculate the merger stat control premium may actually overstate the premium, because the methodology used ignores a potential run up in the stock price between the measurement date for the unaffected price and the date of the offer.

So for instance, let's assume that you're analyzing storage sector stocks. If this market sector increased 10 percent over a 60-day period corresponding to the measurement period used for the control premium calculation, then this so-called control premium actually includes a 10 percent premium related to simply an increase in overall market valuations. Obviously you would want to know this if you're using that transaction premium data to benchmark an appropriate premium to apply to another public company. As mentioned before – I've mentioned it a couple of times – I think fairness opinions, and I think when looking at transaction data overall, but particularly control premium data, I think it's very important to consider the motivations behind the acquisition.

I would strongly suggest that the listeners review fairness opinions to review the important factors considered by investment bankers, the seller, and the buyer assessing the merits of a transaction and the purchase price. Again, these are included in proxy filings with the SEC before a transaction is approved by shareholders. Fairness opinions typically describe the value drivers and valuation metrics related to a proposed action. They also include the reasons that both buyer and seller management support the transaction could include a discussion of the nature and magnitude of suspected synergies relevant public company and transaction multiples considered, certainly other control premium data considered, and also discounted cash flow assumptions, which may include various DCF assumptions using various growth rates and discount rates.

Periodically, if both the buyer and seller are public then the proxy will include a description of the analysis performed by the investment bank of the buyer and the seller. In addition to being useful and assessing control premiums this may also be a quick way for an analyst to find a list of potential guideline companies in relevant M&A transactions to consider in valuing a subject company.

As mentioned before, the transaction premium data that you're looking at it's really – we call it control premium, but it's more appropriately described as acquisition premiums, and those acquisition premiums may reflect a whole host of reasons that may be unrelated to control. Certainly some transactions may be more aptly described as strategic control premiums rather than financial control premiums. That's critical if an analyst thinks that the appropriate level of value for a particular valuation is financial control. So it's important to understand that what control premium is telling you.

In addition, it's important to realize that control premiums are an output to the valuation and negotiations that are actually used to determine the purchase price. So again, I think if you look at the fairness opinion that kind of brings it home. I mean it should make common sense to a valuation analyst if it's true. But when you see the type of analysis that is done, the control premium data is just one of many factors that are considered. And I would certainly argue that a control premium wouldn't be a value driver that should be determinative of what an acquirer would actually pay for another company although it may factor into consideration of the reasonableness of the offer price.

One of the factors I had mentioned previously concerned psychological factors and control premiums. As you know, purchase prices are negotiated and ultimately must be approved by a board of directors and shareholders. So the board of directors must get comfortable with the purchase price offered. And they must find a way to actually communicate their comfort level with the offer price that will make sense to investors.

One of the things that's often looked at and described is the purchase price relative to the 52-week high for that particular stock. Recently there's been some academic research related to the potential impact of the 52-week high price to offer prices. There's two particular working papers that I'll refer you to as well as a CFO article. There are these two professors three professors, two of whom are at Harvard, and the other one is at NYU, who have done a study of transactions – 7,500 public company transactions between

1984 and 2007, where the company that was acquired – the target company – was publicly traded. The findings of these researchers, I think, is fairly interesting and potentially could lead to some additional data points that a valuation specialist wants to look at when assessing control premium data.

What the researchers found was that the offer prices are highly influenced by the target's 52-week high stock price. They described it as a psychological anchor a starting point from which actual bid prices do not sufficiently adjust to reflect only current information.

The target's 52-week high exercise has a strong effect on the bidder's offers, offer price, and the use of the 52-week high's reference point by the target shareholder. So I think that's particularly relevant. Then also if we continue down on this slide is described in the *CFO* article basically the findings were that the greater the difference between the 52-week high and the current stock price the higher the premium that bidders actually paid for companies.

The main point of this research is that the 52-week high may actually influence offer prices; and therefore the control premiums that we're observing when we're looking at control premium data.

If we look at the data and the discussion, and the research in a vacuum, it would argue that if you're valuing a public company, let's say you're working with a public company client, and their price is significantly below their 52-week high, then the implication may be that the company would require an offer price that would result in a higher control premium than on average. But you can't look at that in a vacuum. You must consider certainly whether the price decline relative to the 52-week high is due to one or more specific unfavorable events.

This research, although useful and I think very interesting, it doesn't provide a rule of thumb that we can apply and make our life so easy. For example, yesterday I noted that Hewlett Packard announced the acquisition of Palm, and as I'm sure most people know Palm had developed – it's a mobile operating system, and launched two handsets: the Pre and the Pixy. Unfortunately, the sales of those handsets have greatly disappointed everyone, and HP was one of several companies rumored to have an interest in acquiring Palm. The offer price for Palm was $5.70 a share, and it was accepted by the board, and that represented 23 percent premium over the closing price. However, the 52-week high stock price for Palm is $18.09 I think back some time in September or October of 2009.

Clearly in this case a simple citation of the 52-week high without analyzing the reasons for the decline in value for the Palm, which have been, I'd say, well-documented, would have lead a valuation specialist to a very wrong estimate of a purchase price necessary to acquire a Palm in a hypothetical transaction. Obviously when we look at the transaction data underlying control premiums it's important to understand that there are many different characteristics of that data that you can search by. I've just listed four of them here, and these factors obviously can be used to screen the transactions let's say if you're using some kind of online database.

The reason why I think it's worth mentioned is because certainly if you use well-defined criteria just for your transactions, you're not only going to gather a more relevant pool of transactions and control premium data, but also you can actually spend more time doing valuation analysis and less time merely trying to gather control premium data.

I'm going to show on the slides that follow some of my analysis related to control premium data, which was done the latter part of 2009. What I did was I performed and analysis of Mergerstat®/BVR Control Premium Study™. And I tried to summarize the content of the database using various criteria. This slide gives the break down of the transactions, which reported positive control premiums so it was roughly 5,800 transactions.

These transactions were categorized, so we have it categorized by range of control premium, which you can see on the left-hand side of the table. Then we have that data further broken down into the buyer type, which have been defined by Mergerstat®. We've got strategic, vertical, horizontal, financial, and conglomerate. From my perspective, the strategic, vertical, and horizontal categories can be combined to reflect transactions that may contain synergies that reflect strategic control level of value and therefore strategic premiums. In fact the vast majority of the observed transactions would fall into these categories.

What's interesting, though, is that if you look in the bottom lower right hand portion of this table, you can see that the distribution of control premiums between what I've called strategic buyers and financial buyers is relatively similar across various magnitudes of control premiums. In other words the control premiums measured don't appear to differ greatly in aggregate between types of buyer, at least in terms of some sort of average control premium. Another factor to consider is that I think it's easier to target transactions that could potentially possess elements of strategic control value. But according to Damodaran, again, in "The Value of Control" paper, one potential indicator of financial control premiums would be transactions characterized as hostile.

So I did look at that as well, however, my review of the Mergerstat®/BVR Control Premium Study™ found that there were fewer than 50 transactions that actually were characterized as hostile. So there aren't enough transactions perhaps to really do a lot of analysis along those lines. Another factor to consider possibly would be whether managers were retained post-transaction, because certainly I would argue that the retention of management would likely indicate that there's no sort of financial control premium that current management was mismanaging the business. However, because management is here, it's not uncommon for senior management to be cut as a cost savings synergy post transaction. I don't think that because management was removed is necessarily an indicator that the transaction was that there's some sort of element of financial control premium potentially involved.

The next way that I'm showing you that I looked at the data was by stock exchange. I didn't it for all stock exchanges, but in this analysis I'm simply showing it based upon companies listed on either US or Canadian stock exchanges. What I think this data shows is that potentially an analyst will want to consider stock exchange in sorting the control premium data.

Certainly it's possible that the type of exchange for a company would affect not only company characteristics due to listing requirements by a particular exchange, but also the efficiency of the market price based upon a company that's listed on a particular exchange. So as a result if we look at the data, it's perhaps not surprising that the New York Stock Exchange listed companies who were all acquired at the lowest average control premium while the OTC targeted companies were part of the highest.

So what does this mean? Well, I would say that potentially that if you're applying the control premium to an NYSE listed company that it may be meaningful to choose control premiums obtained from transactions involved with other NYSE companies. So one issue that comes up periodically is what does the control premium represent, or how should it be measured? Should it be measured in terms of equity or something more along the lines of entity value, because certainly most of what I've talked about before and referred to relates to basically equity, control premiums in terms of equity?

Certainly a method of calculating control premium in terms of equity as I described is the unadjusted equity risk premium – or I'm sorry – unadjusted equity control premium. That's the premium that you're going to see reported by Mergerstat and other data sources, and certainly in practice it's what most analysts use.

The second and third methods however are based upon the premise that any sort of premiums for control whether they be financial or strategic really relate more to the overall value of the business, and the overall cash flow generating ability of a business. Therefore when measuring a control premium you should be referencing to some sort of measure of entity value. There's also – I talk about it in a research paper that I've wrote, but certainly in the responses to the appraisal foundation working group, some of which Andrew Fargason is going to talk about later in this presentation, there's pretty good coverage of this issue in some of those responses. In terms of trying to answer this question, I think this chart that I present in this slide kind of shows the impact of how you measure control premium could be significant in terms of the resulting magnitude of the premium.

A simple example, which I'll just – read the first sentence. For example, assume that a company with an invested capital of $100 is acquired for $120 or a 20 percent control premium to invested capital. If we look at the table we can see no matter what the capital structure is if we look at the column for invested capital control premium, it's a 20 percent control premium. However, if we look at the column for equity control premium the level of debt capital and therefore equity capital in the capital structure has a significant impact on the control premium being measured. There's a real potential concern to me that of potentially using control premium data that's based upon a certain capital structure that differs greatly from the capital structure of say a public company that's under valuation.

In terms of trying to analyze this, try to answer this question, I endeavored to analyze the Mergerstat database and see what the data said, because typically in the past periodically when appropriate I've measured the control premium and supported it in terms of invested capital. However, one of the challenges that I would hear let's say during audit review, would be, "Hey, I understand the theory, what you're saying, but you've got to show me some sort of research supporting the use of an investment capital control premium. So that's what I attempted to do – was ultimately create some sort of research that would support that sort of methodology. The premise that I followed was to calculate dollar control premiums based upon the underlying data, and then compare those dollar control premiums paid to the level of equity and then the level of investment capital for that same company.

I calculated the mean and standard deviations of the percentage premiums to equity invested capital respectively and then categorized those measurements based upon different capital structures, which I'll show on the following slide. The measure that I used in determining which was perhaps the better measurement was coefficient of variation and coefficient of variation you simply divide standard deviation by the mean. The basic interpretation is that the measurements that reflect a lower coefficient of variation are those with the least dispersion around their respective means and therefore may be better indicators in this case of the premium paid.

In fact, as I'll show on the slides that follow by measuring the data in this way I was able to find that the premium data actually supports the notion that the benefits of control are based upon factors tied to the value of an entity. This is actually shown in more detail in the paper referred to at the bottom of this slide. So what I'll show you. I'll try to do it quickly here is there are three tables that will show. The first table here if you look at the left hand side of this table, we see debt to total capital and it ranges from zero to 100 percent. So that's how I attempted to categorize the data and then compare based upon transactions, following in the appropriate debt to total capital category. Compare the coefficient of variation for an equity based control premium to that of an invested capital based control premium.

As shown on the right hand side here, in almost every case, the equity coefficient of variation is not lower than the invested capital coefficient of variation, which means that there's less variability if you measure a control premium in terms of invest capital. For some of the debt levels it obviously varies in terms of how much lower it is. But I think those results are fairly significant and kind of prove the theory from my perspective or my interpretation of the data. If we go to the next slide, this is table one real quickly, it's a measurement of the data from all industries all countries in terms of target countries and all buyer types.

Table two is formatted similarly, however it focuses only on US target companies. Again, the data results are similar. Let's see if we go to the third table here, same format again, but this is focused on more strategic type deals, and again the conclusions are the same. The challenge, I found is trying to segregate this data in doing this sort of analysis into more homogeneous groups lets say by industry is that there may not be adequate transaction volumes to generate a meaningful coefficient of variation analysis. But I've no reason to believe that if we were able to do that data with a meaningful sample size that the conclusions wouldn't be the same.

In terms of current practice, in my experience, and certainly reviewing the responses received by the appraisal foundation-working group is that current practice seems to be that theoretically firms can appreciate the invested capital merits, and why theoretically that would make more sense. But they also certainly indicate that in practice they see equity control premiums more commonly. As long as there aren't drastic differences between the companies under analysis, drastic differences in the capital structures that it may not matter in terms of how you do the analysis. But I would argue that it's certainly something that you'll want to consider when using this data in the future.

Again, here I'm going to kind of skip over some of this stuff that goes into more specifics related to using control premium in financial reporting engagements. Again, I think the bottom line is in financial reporting engagements as long as your analysis of market participants leads you to believe that that market participants may include strategic buyers, then it may be appropriate to factor in strategic control benefits in the valuation analysis that you're performing if the underlying economics of the company you're valuing make it appropriate to do so. Some of the financial reporting stuff; financial reporting literature does mention control premiums, but certainly just because there is a mention of control premium by FASB does not mean that FASB is saying that a control premium would always be appropriate in every instance.

Lastly, I'll end my portion of the presentation talking very quickly about some of the SEC views. I think the SEC views on control premiums can be summarized as follows: there is no rule of thumb: you must document the basis for an adjustment for market cap value; and more documentation may be needed. I guess the higher the adjustment to market cap value, the more documentation that you may need.

Here there's just some quotes here from two speeches from two different SEC staff members. Finally I'll just close by saying also if you look at SEC comment letters to specific SEC registrants, the comments in those letters are very, I would say, consistent with their views that have been voiced in these various speeches. So that's the end of my formal presentation. With that I'll turn it over to Mark.

Mark Edwards: Great. Thank you, Brad, for those informative comments. Good afternoon everyone. It's really a treat to be with all of you today. What I'd like to do is add a little more perspective and color on some of the items that Brad has brought up to our attention. I'd like to do this really from two perspectives. The first perspective is that I, like most of you, served in one role in my profession as preparer of valuation analyses that are then reviewed by external auditors and debated and resolved on a number of these issues.

But secondly, I think I can also add some perspective to this group is the other function I serve in our practice is someone who reviews. I suspect some of the work that many on this particular teleconference might prepare, as well as other firms. What we have is kind of a blended body of knowledge that I'd like to share with you some of the best practices that we've observed in that process.

I would also like to point that it's also my privilege that I'm a current member of the ASCPA task force. Our objective is to finish drafting a practice aid, which would be a new one that's dedicated to all of the issues surrounding impairment whether it be goodwill, indefinite lived assets or finite lived assets. We don't have any resolutions, of course, at this point. But what I can tell you is all of the issues surrounding control premiums or cost savings, and how we get from market cap to a concluded value for an impairment testing. Certainly all of these items are on the table and being discussed in some depth.

Then I just want to echo one of the things that Brad mentioned a couple of slides ago is that certainly we acknowledge the footnote. You all have to forgive me, because I am codification-challenged still at this point, so I tend to revert back to the old FASB references. But it certainly was Footnote 16 under FAS 142, which really highlights the fact that a fair value used for impairment testing, may in fact reflect some elements of control that would indicate a price higher than what we could observe in the market. Despite that footnote I would like to echo that again from having my audit hat on that that's not a license to apply an automatic premium in all cases.

I would certainly encourage all of us consider facts and circumstances before we conclude on either whether a premium is relevant or the magnitude of that premium. A couple of other observations before we get into this, and I've got a little case study that's somewhat simplistic, but I think will drive these points home. First of all let's all be careful to remember unit of account and unit valuation. Obviously, in a 142 or a 350 scenario we're talking about a controlling interest, and a 141 the IRR calculations that we all come up with are typically control interests and may also reflect some unique synergistic elements. So that's another unit account, unit of valuation.

Of course, when we look to individual intangible assets underneath the acquisition for purposes of doing the purchase price allocation then we're back to a unit of valuation of the specific asset level. Lastly, for any of us that are involved in the share base payments arena that is typically, again depending on facts and circumstances, going to be a minority non-marketable basis. So whether premiums or in some cases discounts are relevant I think let's all remember that it always depends on what the starting point is and what the premise of value that you're starting with. So it's important that was we assemble these values and review them that we keep that in mind.

Just a couple of comments on reconciliations, and I wish that we would have in our survey, and hindsight is 20/20. But I would have liked to have known how many folks as part of performing impairment services for their clients actually go through this process when it's a public company. I think just the terminology point here is that most of the literature that I'm reading on this particular topic now is transitioning not to the word "reconciliation" but the word "comparison."

So I'd like to take just a couple of minutes and talk about why we think that's important. I know that we perform this on all of our outbound engagements. For the inbound engagements that we're reviewing from an audit perspective we typically prefer to see this in some form just to demonstrate that someone's thought through how the conclusions for impairment testing may reconcile or compare to external observable indications market value as well.

The benefits that we see performing this exercise is clearly an analytic that can be used by this valuation specialist to test reasonableness. Perhaps identify issues that need more thought, more discussion more inquiry. Perhaps it could identify a calculation error that needs to be revised. So it's a good analytic tool. It gives us a way to test the reasonableness of the outcome and the conclusion that will be used for impairment testing. And from my perspective as an auditor it's pretty good audit evidence to have that in there and certainly something, again, I think I mentioned earlier, that we look for in a review capacity.

One other area that it has helped, and again this is just an observation from practice, is sometimes one of the more contentious issues in impairment testing for goodwill is in a multiunit environment and how you go about allocating assets and liabilities down to specific units and invariably there's some amount left over in what we'll call unit X or the corporate unit.

By comparing this to a parallel reconciliation of carrying values, it may help us identify those situations where there may not be an apples-to-apples comparison in terms of the carrying value that's being tested; and the fair value – corresponding fair value that's being calculated. So it's a good tool. A good process we think of best practice, and I would encourage anybody that's not going through the steps to think about doing that forward.

The question that comes up a lot is, what happens with private companies, and do they get a pass on this reconciliation or comparison? I think the short answer to that is no. But only for the purpose of doing the analytics and reasonableness test that we just mentioned on the last slide. Now, that's easy to say obviously, but in this case we are obviously absent, and arm's length sale of this business last night or this morning. We really don't have an observable external market price from which to conduct this comparison or reconciliation.

Therefore, again from practice what we see there's really two ways you can do it. The most egregious way is to do fair value of everything and try to fit it together, but I think it's rare that we find time and or budget to do that in all cases. So I would say at a minimum again facts and circumstances.

This is really a time where I would recommend that you would engage on a proactive basis the external auditor and discuss these issues in advance. It makes the process go a lot smoother and more efficient. But try to understand how much clearance there may be. Try to understand what materiality may be. Try to understand if there's some units that don't have any goodwill in them that are components of value of the total company, and see if there's some way to do some analytics, some comparable multiples, some implied cap rates. Apply any of our valuation tools to come up with enough audit evidence at the end of the day to say, "Well, we've got it covered A, B, and C, and so we think overall it's reasonable." Again, I think that is something that we need to think about even in the situation where we're doing private companies.

A couple of comments here and then I also want to share some new thinking that I've come across on some circles of late. This is a very simple P x Q formula here, but I just want to make sure that we think about some of the other variables that may be involved here. One is that let's be sure that we remember to look at the capital structure to see if there's some other elements of capital there, and particularly preferred stock or some other type of equity holding that needs to get factored ingot the total equity picture. A couple of words of caution if I could, and I don't know how many of us have read statement 160. Again, I apologize, I can't tell you where to find it in the codification, but if you have the cross over tool you'll find it.

In 160, I believe it was paragraph 839 that talks about a way on a post-141(r) basis to conduct impairment testing. Basically what it says is when you're calculating the fair in step one follow the rules that are in 141(r), or in this case I do know that's 805. For those of you not familiar with that particular guidance, it basically says that the cost to be allocated and in this case the cost to be aggregated in determining the fair value in step one is three components. It's the consideration paid or the fair value of the interest owned, assuming that's a control interest. Then two more blocks, the first was any non-controlling interest that may be there, and in the case of 141 it would be any previously held interest in the company. So the ramification there is we will now, henceforth be doing impairment testing in utilizing 100 percent or almost 100 percent of cash flows in calculating step one values.

So my points all to this group is when we're calculating the starting point to do this reconciliation or comparison if we just do P x Q with a traded price, we're only going to be picking up the controlling interest's fair value. So for purposes of doing this test, it's important that we add back the fair value of the non-controlling interests or else we'll have an apples and oranges comparison in our reconciliation efforts. Then one other issue that you may come across and that is with those companies that have what I'll call old 141-type minority interests. There, for example, if I bought 80 percent of a company I would have allocated 80 percent of the assets and liabilities, and the minority interest would have come over at book value.

The result being that goodwill represents 80 fair value, 20 percent historical costs, and you can imagine that as you get down to maybe a 60 percent owner percentage that the gap widens. What happens under this new 160 is that you still would calculate the step one value in accordance of the guidance 141(r), which would mean almost 100 percent of cash flows, and you would be comparing that to a carrying value that does not reflect a full step up of the goodwill. That's a transition issue. It creates cushion for those companies that have again what I'll call old minority interests, as opposed to new non-controlling interests. I know that's a lot to chew on, but wanted to be sure I put that on the table because that's a live issue in current exercises in companies that non-controlling interests.

We mentioned some of these in Brad's presentation, control synergies. Control premiums have a lot of stuff in them. Again, from an audit perspective, I think – and again I'll speak personally. This is my preference that when I review these I really prefer to see a quantitative decomposition of why the specialist in management thinks that there is some level of value above what we can observe in the trading price. We prefer quantitative, quite frankly, because it can be audited easier, and we think it requires a very diligent discipline discussion with clients to help come up with some of these inputs that need to be analyzed and preferably quantified.

In addition, there are obviously some qualitative items that we have talked about previously. That would be pink sheeted, thinly traded, low float, large blocks of family ownership, any number of those things that would make us think that perhaps the traded price may not be the best indication of value, but I would caution all of us on this teleconference to remember that it's not a good position to go to an external auditor and say, "Because of these things we simply did not consider an external indication of value." I think you'll find that to be a non-starter with a lot of our firms.

Not that it's determinative, but according to Burt Fox's comments that Brad mentioned a few slides back is that it's going to be imperative that if you have a situation that's suggestive of a very wide gap between an observed price and a concluded fair value for impairment testing, all I'm saying to this group is it's very important to have good, good documentation. So what we'll do here is I've got a very simplistic case study we can go through, and just one way that you might think about quantifying some of these things.

Again, here's our company. It's a public company XYZ; trades at $3.50, market cap of $4.2 million, and what we'll further assume is that there's good volume, good float. We assume that that is a good liquid price.

So the acquire believes the redundant costs would allow the new company to pick up about 50 basis points in margin, and we think that the savings is permanent, not temporary. But we also know they're about to launch a new product that will enhance their profits as shown in the DCF that they gave to us and management's PFI includes the revenues, expenses and profit of this new product line. But they've also told us that this information has not been disclosed through any public filings or press releases. In this case, we do have a non-controlling interest of 16.7 percent, so not too bad there.

The first thing we have, these next two slides, and you'll forgive me for making this as simplistic as I can to hopefully get it to fit on these slides. But let me just highlight what you can see as there is a core revenue, and then here's some new product revenue, and some new product that we can see start slow and then grows to somewhat substantial levels as we get out into the terminal period. Then the next slide after this is basically the bottom half of the DCF where we make our cash flow adjustments. The beauty of creating slides for presentations like these is we can assume away a lot of complexities. We've determined a WACC of 14 percent and a fair value of the enterprise of $8.7 million in this case.

Point here is that the $8.7 million reflects core revenues as well as new product revenues and earnings. The first study here is, well, maybe we can quantify these cost savings. So all we do is we say that there's combined revenue of $10.5 million, and the savings is 50 basis point on the $10.5 million tax-affected. Run it through a DCF. Again, we're including a terminal value here, because of the representation that these cost savings would be permanent. So you want to be sure when discussing these items and gathering facts that you're going to use in the analysis that you'll be sure to talk about things like that. Is it permanent, etc?

The other thing I want to point out is you'll see that the WACC here is higher, 18 percent, and that's in recognition of even if these are just cost savings. These are anticipated cost savings. We probably all are familiar that one of the more difficult things of integrating or one of the reasons that companies fail or don't do as well after they're subject to the acquisition or mergers, because the integration doesn't go as smoothly as possible, so a little bit higher discount rate here to recognize that fact. Here's another one. Well, we've got this asymmetric data that again is not reflected in the public, and therefore the argument is not reflective in the share price, and so therefore in this particular DCF we've broken out the EBITDA revenue associated just with that new product line, and discount of that back. It's something a little higher than the WACC. WACC was 14. This is 15.

Again, there's probably a little bit more risk baked in this forecast and the core revenues. Certainly some judgment is involved here, but the point is we're trying to get to a point where we can say that there's a $1.8 million of our $8.7 million is reflective of the new product that's not known to the public. If I back up one slide, we're saying of the $8.7 million that we calculated, about $300,000 of that is associated with what we think is cost savings synergies. Here's the balance sheet. I may make a correction to the carrying value. I think that should be $4.5 million to reflect the NCI. So excuse me for that.

Then we get to the reconciliation of the comparison, and simply we do this in two steps. Here's an enterprise value that's from the first DCF we saw. This debt of $1.5 million from the balance sheet we just looked at, which means we haven't applied a fair value of equity of $4.2 million compared with a market cap of equity of $4.2 million.

At first glance that applies a premium of 71.4 percent. Now, we in our group certainly don't, we don't subscribe to any bright lines as well. But I can just tell you honestly that I saw 70 percent premium, I would get a bit nervous and say, "Well, can you help me explain the difference." Below here is what we're trying to demonstrate with that is we've got $4.2 million in market cap, but we think $300,000 of that is related to the asymmetric impact – or excuse me, the cost savings. Another $1.8 million is related to the asymmetric impact.

Here's this element here that again I wanted to show you that again the $3.50 share price doesn't reflect the value that's inuring to the non-controlling interest. We've added that back, and it reflects a 10 percent discount. We can debate the merits of the 10 percent discount on the next BVR presentation, but why that's not a flat number is because it reflects a little discount. What we would argue is that we've accounted for a little over $7 million of value, which leaves about 144 unexplained. Again, from an audit perspective, I would look that's 3 percent of market cap, 2 percent of concluded equity, and at that point I would probably say, "We're done," and ask for a final report, and we'd write our memo, and that would be it at that point.

That is the couple of comments and observations that I learned through the practice aid task force as well as observing worked on by others, and comments that we've received from primarily the big four reviewing our work. Thank you very much for your time. And, Blake, I'll turn it over to you and Andrew.

Andrew Fargason: Thank you, Mark, and thanks guys. My piece of this is not going to be all that long, and so I'm hoping that we will have some time to get to questions if you guys want to send them in, and that's mainly because I really did not join the panel in order to do more technical exposition like that that Brad and Mark have both done very well for us here on the call to this point. Instead, I was asked to join because of my participation with the Appraisal

Foundation's current Working Group on Control Premiums, and update you on that group's progress. Certainly no conclusions have been reached at this point, so my participation is not any kind of endorsement of anything that's been said. Although, I think the guys did a good job of surveying the landscape, and saying what's out there, and how it's been done.

But rather just to sort of update you that there is this Working Group, what the Working Group is, and how you might want to provide us information, give us some input, etc as we're still in deliberations. In general I think this piece of the presentation comes on the heals of an explanation of what the reconciliation process, or as Mark says, probably a better term comparison process, which is a term I like better, too; because really the Working Group was formed, I think, mostly in response to what most of the people on the call probably went through back in late '08 early '09, which was the sort of massive impairment write down process, where it felt like we wrote down all the goodwill that was out there on public companies on the market.

In doing that, I think we all came to realize, and certainly those of you doing a lot of audit review on it, and those of us doing the work realize there is certainly a variance of practice, and some fairly distinctive diversity of control practice and control premiums. When we turned around to ask ourselves after the market tanked, and we're doing then 142 testing, we add up our reporting in at values and we want to compare it to the public traded price.

So what's a reasonable control premium? I'm not sure that the methodologies that were in place went down all that well in a lot of cases with auditors particularly in terms of auditability. It is a tough issue. So that's one of the, I think, prime drivers of why the appraisal foundation formed a working group. So just a little background on the working groups, and then I'll tell you how you can provide us with some input if you chose to do so, and we would encourage you to do that.

There are currently three working groups overseen by the Appraisal Foundation's Task Force on Valuations and Financial Reporting also called the VFR. Some of you may be familiar with these. The first one it started up, I believe, in '08, maybe even earlier than that, and has issued an exposure draft. It's on contributory asset charges.

There is a second working group on valuation of customer related assets, and I believe a big part of the deliberations there will be on the access earnings method, I would imagine. And a lot of the diversity in practice that certainly that issue has involved in it. The third group is the one I'm on, which is control premiums.

Because that group is so specifically involved with the exact topic of this panel, it seemed to those of us on the group that our participation was warranted, but it didn't seem appropriate for me to get on and make any direct comments about methodology, because we really frankly haven't decided on a lot of these issues.

Although I will say that nothing that Brad or Mark just went through jumped out at me as something dramatically different from what we're deliberating. These are certainly all things that are under consideration, and I'll touch on some questions that we have out to the public in a minute. The purpose of these working groups is to establish best practices for valuations and financial reporting, develop some guidance hopefully with some good input from lots of practitioners.

The participants tend to be both independent valuation firms and accounting firms of all sizes. So I think we've got good knowledgeable people participating. And if we can get some buy in some of these issues I think it will certainly help in consistency and certainly help in reviews going forward, specifically relative to working group three. We do have representatives from three of the big four, and then Mercer and myself from American Appraisal on the group. Started working in July of '09, and we expect to issue an exposure draft I would say this year.

This process, as you can imagine, is fairly laborious. We've had a number of meetings in person, and a number of meetings by phone, and you can dig into some of these issues for a very long time with people who like to talk value and who like these issues. We're addressing control premiums in the fair value accounting setting only.

So it is a very US fair value financial reporting centric analysis. Now, that's not to say that we think there are or there are not big differences between fair value for US GAAP and fair market value for, let's say federal tax. We haven't decided what comments to make about that, whether to say, "There may be. We haven't addressed it, or we think there are some, or we don't believe there are any. We're just discussing it." So I really don't know how we'll address that, or in what depth we'll address it.

Some of the general topics, though, just the scope of our work are terms and definitions. So you look at things like words that have been thrown around here, control premium, versus acquisition premium, versus transaction premium, and again there's another day's conversation with a group of technical people who do this for a living. So there's a lot of things that we're trying to hash out in terms of what's important, and what's not, and what some of the terms ought to be, and what the definitions ought to be.

Certainly the theoretical concepts underlying these issues we'll do some exposition of those, and a lot of the documentation that's been provided with this webinar is the same stuff we're looking at. It's the same things that are out there in the public domain that have been submitted, and then what our best practice is for measurement.

Obviously, no rule of thumb is going to come out of it. There's going to be a lot of facts and circumstances to consider, but we do want to try to come up with some, not rules but measurement best practice-type guidance. So one of the main points I wanted to get on and make is that we do have a request for comments out there, and I think the people that are involved in this call today would be a good group to send us comments if you were so inclined.

Some of you already have. We issued it a while ago, back in December, and the deadline for submissions has passed, but certainly we're still considering whatever comes in. So there's no problem in submitting that. We do want to gather input in this request for comments, just on a certain few initial questions that came up that we wanted to see what the diversity of practice was. So don't misconstrue the questions to be that we're thinking one way or the other, and tell us if you think we're right or wrong. We're simply asking what are you doing in these areas to make sure that we cover the waterfront, that we don't get in and kind of get groupthink going, and assume that everyone thinks the same way on a certain issue.

We want to try to draw out some responses, and we've gotten some very good responses. There is some diversity of practice out there. There was a range of answers on a number of items and some consensus on others at least to this point. You can find, just for your information, administratively you can find that request for comments on the Appraisals Foundation website. That's appraisalfoundation.org under the financial reporting piece, and it does include instructions for submitting responses to us.

We'll take everything you want to send. We've gotten very long ones and very short ones, so anything you want to send, and the responses that we've received to date are posted at the same location, and some of those are fairly interesting if you're facing issues on this, and you want to know. Some of you may have joined to try to guide where this issue goes, because you have an open job right now. You're just trying to figure out an answer, and there may be some good information in there for you to kind of survey what's going on out there, and see what practice is, and what the range of practice is right now.

The questions that are in there are, or the areas for comment that are listed in there just briefly. I don't want to try to talk about these at this point, because we're fairly well out of time. I don't know if we have questions we want to talk about or not, but I want to leave some time if I can. But we've got six issues in there for comment, applicability of control premium to public market share price. There is a range there. Some people believe it's not even applicable. You shouldn't be using it all the way to, yeah, there should be a control premium added to sort of P x Q price times quantity on public market every time, so comments on your thinking there. Negative control premiums, is there any theoretical basis for them? Do you ever see them? We just wanted to throw that out and see what comments we got back.

Calculation methods, and the next few questions were trying to collect the sort of methods to make sure we don't miss something good out there. I'll say to date we haven't found anything new under the sun, but we're looking. The calculation method traditional equity method versus tick method is one. And that's something that's already been commented on I think fairly well that there are cases that the tick method may be needed. Are you using it? Are you not using it? Do you have a strong feeling either way or are you always sticking with traditional equity method etc. Cash flow methods, what methods are you using? When we say cash flow methods, what do you hear and what do you mean by it when you use that term? What other methods are in use for measuring control premiums, a catchall to make sure we don't miss anything. And then some questions and comments on use of comparable transactions to find out what's going on out there in the market.

And I think that's it. I just want to encourage everybody to go on that website and send us comments still if you want even though it says the deadline's past, and then look for the document for public comment that'll be available as soon as we get through the process.

Blake Lyman: Well, thank you very much Andrew. This is Blake again. We are over time, but I think if we have the availability of our speakers who might like to address a couple of questions here as well as in writing as I said.

I'd also like to remind our viewers that the documents that Andrew referenced, the call for submissions, and some of those that have already been posted are linked from our reading page from today's conference. So please find them either there or at the Appraisal Foundation Website.

To our panel, we have quite a few questions that have come in and obviously since we're out of time, I'd like to know if there are some specific questions, which you all would like to address in just a few moments here.

Brad Pursel: Yeah, Blake, this is Brad Pursel. I think it wasn't really a question but a comment, and perhaps – I'll say a misinterpretation or misreading of the first survey question. The first survey question that we asked was do you always apply control premiums in, I think, it's goodwill impairment testing when you're valuing a publicly traded company, let's say. And so the question was, do you always?

I don't want people on the call to interpret no to mean never. So that just means that people are saying they don't always apply one. Even though I would also have answered that question no, because I don't always apply one, because I don't always think a control premium is appropriate. I just wanted to make sure that there wasn't any misunderstanding of the survey what it was asking or the survey results, because most people did answer that no. That was one thing I wanted to address.

There was another question I saw related to referencing to one of my slides that mentioned referred to high volatility or unusual levels of volatility and how that might indicate that the stock price isn't necessarily undervalued, but just maybe it doesn't reflect fair value. And just my thoughts there were again if we think back to the extreme volatility of capital markets during certain periods of time of the fourth quarter of 2008. I mean, I can just recall a particular company's stock that I was valuing, doing the impairment testing for credible impressive levels of volatility one day to the next, and so in doing the valuation for impairment testing the big four auditor in that case was comfortable with us looking at other indications of value of besides just the impairment test date stock price.

So we looked at a range. We looked at a 30-day. We looked at a five-day. We looked at various ranges just because that level of volatility was so unprecedented.

Blake Lyman: And in the time we have remaining is there anything else that we'd like to address?

Andrew Fargason: Yeah, this is Andrew Fargason and we did have a question from Eric Nath. Hello, Eric. I'm going to read it, Eric, and then answer it as best I can, and obviously I'm not going to go into to too much detail. But I do think I can answer the question.

It says, "This question is for Andrew. Is there any consideration by the working group to simply say that application of control premiums is the wrong way to go? And the differences of valuation between public market price and the aggregate of the underlying values of the various reporting units needs to focus on more fundamental reasons for the differences as opposed to how to best apply a control premium."

Frankly, I think the answer is yes, Eric. The first part of your question gave me a little bit of pause, but I think I understand it. I think what you're saying, and sorry we're not actually having a back and forth conversation is are you considering something besides just saying, "Well, we've got these underlying reporting units. Apply a control premium of X and voilà, I get to the answer." And, yeah, I think there is a lot more to it than that. There has to be. I don't actually think to use your terms that's necessarily the right way to go, literally meaning bottom up as opposed to saying – and I think this was more what was presented over the course of this webinars by the guys was, it's a comparison. You look at what the public market value is. That's a fact.

You go in, you value these reporting units, you get your answer, and then you're saying – and I think is where I probably agree with you, because it's what the end of your question sounds like it's recommending a focus on more fundamental reasons for those differences. I do think that the audit firms are requiring particularly where it's critical, the pass-fail issue, etc, this sort of poster child case of the 20 percent premium, implied premium, you would pass, and the 15 you would fail. In other words you're right on the border. When you add it up, maybe you pass, but you imply a difference of we'll call it 30 percent, and can you get there or not, etc.

I think you have to dig down. The idea that you're going to say that's fine, because we simply calculate a control premium of 25. Apply it to the sum of our – well, either the equity or the tick. Or recalculate it. Apply it to some of those reporting units, and we get there. I think there's a lot more to it than that. And actually coming at it from the other direction is the way we're probably going to have to support it in the future, which is why do you have a difference, and the guys talked about a whole number of things, all of which we're talking about in the group. By no means is this a settled issue. And, Eric, your papers have definitely been a part of the discussion and a fairly big part, and I think you've had some discussions with the guys on the group as well, which I think is good. So hopefully that helps.

Blake Lyman: Well, clearly no resolution today, but part of the ongoing discussion of control premiums. We'll have to call it time now. We're just five minutes to the top of the hour. As I said we'll solicit some response from our speakers in writing that we'll post to our reading page, and send out an announcement of that.

This will conclude today's presentation. Of course, BVR would like to thank Brad Pursel, Mark Edwards, and Andrew Fargason for their expertise, and all of our listeners for attending.

Transcripts and recordings of this and all teleconferences are available for purchase via our on-demand packs. You can find more information on conference-on-demand packs at bvresources.com/training, where you can also find more information on future BVR teleconferences, webinars, and live events.

Control Premiums: Applications and Analysis

BVR
What It's Worth

Business Valuation Resources, LLC
(888) 287-8258 or (503) 291-7963
www.BVResources.com

Brad Pursel
CPA/ABV, CFA, ASA | Brown Smith Wallace LLC
Mark Edwards
CPA/ABV, CFA | Grant Thornton, LLP
Andrew Fargason
CFA | American Appraisal

© 2010, Business Valuation Resources, LLC

Send questions to:
TC-Questions@BVResources.com

Overview of Presentation Agenda

- **Prepared Presentations**
  - Brad Pursel
    - Overview of Various Control Premium Issues
    - Discussion of Control Premium Data
  - Mark Edwards
    - Issues Unique to Control Premiums under Financial Reporting
    - Cash Flow-Based Measures of Control Premiums
  - Andrew Fargason
    - Discussion regarding The Appraisal Foundation's Working Group on Control Premiums Best Practices for Financial Reporting
- **Q&A Session**

2

Send questions to: TC-Questions@BVResources.com

© 2010, Business Valuation Resources, LLC

Control Premiums: Applications and Analysis

Before we begin...

- Some basics regarding our presentation on control premiums
  - **Theoretical Debate**
    - Some analysts argue that the application of a control premium should be rarely used (if ever). For the purposes of our presentation, we have assumed that a control premium may be appropriate to use in certain circumstances.
  - **No "Rule of Thumb"**
    - The application of a control premium is facts and circumstances specific and there would be instances where we would not apply a control premium. In other words, the acceptance of the control premium concept does not mean that it's applicability in every valuation engagement is a "given".
    - Impossible to provide a comprehensive "rule of thumb" that will dictate the magnitude of an appropriate control premium.

3

BVR Send questions to: TC-Questions@BVResources.com

© 2010, Business Valuation Resources, LLC

Control Premiums: Applications and Analysis

Before we begin... (Cont.)

- **Applicability of Control Premiums**
  - Although much of our discussion will be focused on financial reporting applications, we believe that there is general applicability of most of the concepts discussed to other valuation purposes.
  - We will consider the following two potential applications of control premium data:
    - Adjust a public company client's market cap upwards for purposes of goodwill impairment testing; and
    - Adjust guideline public company comparable company market caps upward for purposes of estimating applicable market multiples to be used in valuation of client (public or private).

4

BVR Send questions to: TC-Questions@BVResources.com

© 2010, Business Valuation Resources, LLC

Control Premiums: Applications and Analysis

Brad Pursel

- Overview of Various Control Premium Issues
- Discussion of Control Premium Data

5

© 2010, Business Valuation Resources, LLC

Overview of Control Premiums

- **Some definitions**
  - **Control premium** is defined as follows: "an amount or a percentage by which the pro rata value of a controlling interest exceeds the pro rata value of a noncontrolling interest in a business enterprise to reflect the power of control." (Source: International Glossary of Business Valuation Terms).
  - **Control** is defined as "the power to direct the management, dominate the decision making process and set the policies of a business enterprise." (Source: International Glossary of Business Valuation Terms).
  - Two potential types of control premium:
    - **Financial** - Premium relates to the potential to increase cash flows and/or lower risk for subject company by changing how business is managed (either currently or at some point in the future).
    - **Strategic** - Premium depends upon combination with another firm to increase cash flows and/or lower risk via synergies.

6

© 2010, Business Valuation Resources, LLC

Overview of Control Premiums (Cont.)

- **What is the importance of distinguishing between financial control and strategic control?**
  - Control premium studies are often based upon acquisitions where often the premiums paid are tied to factors such as expected synergies stemming from combination with another firm (strategic control)
  - Strategic control premium data may provide a poor benchmark to the value to be generated from merely obtaining control over the subject firm and operating optimally on a stand-alone basis (financial control).
  - **As with any use of control premium data, remember that the data is biased towards companies that were perceived to be good acquisition candidates.**

7

BVR Send questions to: TC-Questions@BVResources.com

© 2010, Business Valuation Resources, LLC

Control Premiums: Applications and Analysis

Overview of Control Premiums (Cont.)

- **Methods of measuring value attributable to control (strategic or financial)**
  1. **Quantifying cash flows** attributable to control by considering actions that could be taken to optimally manage a firm and/or synergistic benefits to be obtained from combining with another firm.
  2. **Applying transaction multiples** that reflect the value paid to similar entities.
  3. **Applying a control premium** to values considered to be on a noncontrolling interest basis, such as a public company's market cap.

8

BVR Send questions to: TC-Questions@BVResources.com

© 2010, Business Valuation Resources, LLC

Control Premiums: Applications and Analysis

Underlying Assumptions

- The application of a control premium assumes the following:
  1. Public company share price understates the value of 100% of equity due to one or more of the following:
     a. Prices are on a minority interest basis (i.e., includes an embedded discount for lack of control) and must be adjusted to state the value on a control basis.
     b. Current share price does not accurately measure the fair value of a minority interest.
     c. Nature of the public company is such that it is possible that a merger with another company would generate synergies (for example, lower costs and/or higher revenues). However, with the exception of an investment value standard, the value must not include entity-specific synergies.

9

Send questions to: TC-Questions@BVResources.com

© 2010, Business Valuation Resources, LLC

Control Premiums: Applications and Analysis

Underlying Assumptions (Cont.)

2. Assumes that a valuation specialist can quantify a reasonable premium to the public company share price (or changes to the public company cash flows), which may include an analysis of the following:
   a. Subject company trading history (for example, 52-week price data);
   b. Guideline company multiples;
   c. Historical transaction multiples;
   d. Forecasted company cash flows, which may include stand-alone cash flows, synergistic cash flows, and/or cash flows from changing strategies, policies, etc; and
   e. Historical control premium data.
3. Potential buyers exist in the market willing to pay a premium to acquire the public company.

10

Send questions to: TC-Questions@BVResources.com

© 2010, Business Valuation Resources, LLC

Control Premiums: Applications and Analysis

"Our stock is underpriced" or Stock Market Inefficiency

- **Indicators that current stock price may not accurately reflect value of a minority interest in the company:**
  - Periods of high stock price volatility
  - Low float
  - Low trading volume
  - No analyst coverage
  - Asymmetric information
- **Asymmetric information**: management knows information that investing public does not. Examples may include:
  - New product or service launch
  - New customer "win"
  - New market entrance

11

© 2010, Business Valuation Resources, LLC

"Our stock is underpriced" or Stock Market Inefficiency (Cont.)

- **"Bullish" indicators may include:**
  - Positive analyst recommendations (be wary of bias)
  - Stock redemptions
  - Insider purchases
  - Debt capital issuances
- **"Bearish" indicators may include:**
  - Negative analyst recommendations
  - Stock issuances
  - Insider sales
  - Short sales percentage or short interest
- However, neither bullish nor bearish indicators may mean that management or analysts are "right". However, it may be helpful to gather such documentation as work paper support.

12

© 2010, Business Valuation Resources, LLC

Sources of Control Premium Data

- A control premium is calculated as follows:

$$\text{Control Premium} = \frac{(\text{Transaction Price} - \text{Stock Price})}{\text{Stock Price}}$$

  where the stock price is the publicly-traded price preceding the announcement of the acquisition.
- Frequently cited sources for control premium data:
  - Mergerstat® Review – includes tables for historical premium levels by industry.
  - Mergerstat®/BVR Control Premium Database – searchable database using various criteria and downloadable into Excel®.

13

© 2010, Business Valuation Resources, LLC

Analyzing Control Premium Data

- **Does the observed premium data reflect control?**
  - Transactions may capture one or more factors that are unrelated to the value related to financial control and/or strategic control.
    1. Changing suboptimal management policies (financial control only);
    2. Market participant level synergies (strategic control only);
    3. Buyer-specific synergies (may not reflect either financial or strategic control);
    4. Asset that was undervalued by market (neither financial nor strategic control);
    5. Market returns between measurement date and acquisition date;

14

© 2010, Business Valuation Resources, LLC

Analyzing Control Premium Data (Cont.)

- **Does the observed premium data reflect control? (Cont.)**
  6. Asset value already included portion of value attributable to acquisition via information leakage or investor expectations regarding an acquisition;
  7. Stupidity/management hubris (not financial or strategic control);
  8. Negotiation skill (not financial or strategic control); and
  9. Psychological factors.
- Per Dr. Aswath Damodaran, non-control factors to consider in reviewing control premium data includes: information leakage, which impacts measurement of the acquisition premium; motives of buyers, which may include synergies; undervalued stock; and management hubris or "stupid premium." (Source: BVR *Control Premia Teleconference Transcript*, August 24, 2006).

15

BVR Send questions to: TC-Questions@BVResources.com
© 2010, Business Valuation Resources, LLC
Control Premiums: Applications and Analysis

Analyzing Control Premium Data (Cont.)

- **A more accurate description of the observed transaction premiums would be <u>acquisition premiums</u>.**
  - The premium data reported may reflect factors that are unrelated to the benefit obtained from merely managing a company optimally on a stand-alone basis.
- **Control premiums are an <u>output</u> to the valuation and negotiations used to determine purchase price.**
  - Purchase price in transactions is determined by the valuation inputs, such as forecasted cash flows based upon strategy.
  - Stock price levels preceding acquisitions may reflect varying levels of expectations regarding likelihood and benefits to be obtained from a transaction.

16

BVR Send questions to: TC-Questions@BVResources.com
© 2010, Business Valuation Resources, LLC
Control Premiums: Applications and Analysis

Psychological Factors and Implied Control Premiums

- One illustration of the control premium being an output to a more complicated process is recent academic research related to the impact on offer prices of the 52-week high price.
- The impact of the 52-week high price was observed in recent academic research discussed in the following:
  - "The Psychology of Pricing in Mergers and Acquisitions" (May 2009) and "A Reference Point Theory of Mergers and Acquisitions" (December 2009), both working papers by Malcolm Baker (Harvard), Xin Pan (Harvard) and Jeffrey Wurgler (NYU).
  - "Sellers High", *CFO* (July-August 2009), page 17, which discusses the May 2009 working paper.

17

BVR Send questions to: TC-Questions@BVResources.com

© 2010, Business Valuation Resources, LLC

Control Premiums: Applications and Analysis

Psychological Factors and Implied Control Premiums (Cont.)

- "Offer prices are highly influenced by the target's 52-week high stock price. This price likely serves as a *psychological anchor* – a starting point from which actual bid prices do not sufficiently adjust to reflect only current information. I show that <u>the target's 52-week high exercises a strong effect on the bidder's offer price.</u> A number of bidders offer exactly this price...The effect is difficult to square with alternative explanations and appears best explained in terms of the <u>use of the 52-week high as a reference point by the target's shareholders or as an anchor in negotiations with the bidder</u> (emphasis added)." (Source: "The Psychology of Pricing in Mergers and Acquisitions")
- As described in *CFO* , "The study found that <u>more deals were priced at (52-week high) than any other</u>, and <u>offers were more likely to be approved if they exceeded that high, even controlling for the level of the offer premium.</u> In addition, the greater the difference between the 52-week high and the current stock price, the higher the premium that bidders paid for companies (emphasis added)." (Source: "Sellers High")

18

BVR Send questions to: TC-Questions@BVResources.com

© 2010, Business Valuation Resources, LLC

Control Premiums: Applications and Analysis

Psychological Factors and Implied Control Premiums(Cont.)

- Due to the findings that the 52-week high plays a significant role in offer prices (and implied control premiums), it may be useful to compare a public company's current stock price to its 52-week high.
  - If price is significantly below 52-week high, then the implication is that the company may require an offer price that implies a higher control premium.
    - However, consider whether the price decline relative to 52-week high is due to one or more specific unfavorable events.
    - Although 52-week high may be used in assessing an offer, the 52-week high may be irrelevant from a valuation perspective.

19

Send questions to: TC-Questions@BVResources.com

© 2010, Business Valuation Resources, LLC

Control Premiums: Applications and Analysis

Characteristics of Transactions Underlying Control Premium Data

- In conducting an analysis of control premium data, it is important to understand the characteristics of the underlying transactions. Characteristics to consider include:
  - Buyer type (i.e., financial, strategic, etc.), which may introduce buyer-specific assumptions such as synergies
  - Size of interest acquired, which may impact premium paid
  - Transaction date, which may reflect different M&A/stock market conditions
  - Target company stock exchange listing, which may reflect efficiency of market prices

20

Send questions to: TC-Questions@BVResources.com

© 2010, Business Valuation Resources, LLC

Control Premiums: Applications and Analysis

Control Premium Data – Buyer Type Statistics

Snapshot of Mergerstat®/BVR Control Premium Database (as of 11/09)

All Transactions (Positive Control Premiums Only)								
		Buyer Type						
Mergerstat Control Premium	Transaction Count	Strategic	Vertical	Horizontal	Financial	Conglomerate	Strategic / Vertical / Horizontal	Financial / Conglomerate
>=100%	487	163	4	237	76	7	404	83
90% to 99%	109	39	4	55	11	0	98	11
80% to 89%	155	55	1	73	24	2	129	26
70% to 79%	200	76	2	89	31	2	167	33
60% to 69%	317	98	6	156	54	3	260	57
50% to 59%	421	149	4	198	69	1	351	70
40% to 49%	503	196	7	211	85	4	414	89
30% to 39%	780	328	13	320	113	6	661	119
20% to 29%	987	416	10	383	166	12	809	178
10% to 19%	1,021	447	11	353	203	7	811	210
1% to 9%	834	368	5	263	192	6	636	198
Total	5,814	2,335	67	2,338	1,024	50	4,740	1,074
Percentage of Total								
>=100%	100.0%	33.5%	0.8%	48.7%	15.6%	1.4%	83.0%	17.0%
90% to 99%	100.0%	35.8%	3.7%	50.5%	10.1%	0.0%	89.9%	10.1%
80% to 89%	100.0%	35.5%	0.6%	47.1%	15.5%	1.3%	83.2%	16.8%
70% to 79%	100.0%	38.0%	1.0%	44.5%	15.5%	1.0%	83.5%	16.5%
60% to 69%	100.0%	30.9%	1.9%	49.2%	17.0%	0.9%	82.0%	18.0%
50% to 59%	100.0%	35.4%	1.0%	47.0%	16.4%	0.2%	83.4%	16.6%
40% to 49%	100.0%	39.0%	1.4%	41.9%	16.9%	0.8%	82.3%	17.7%
30% to 39%	100.0%	42.1%	1.7%	41.0%	14.5%	0.8%	84.7%	15.3%
20% to 29%	100.0%	42.1%	1.0%	38.8%	16.8%	1.2%	82.0%	18.0%
10% to 19%	100.0%	43.8%	1.1%	34.6%	19.9%	0.7%	79.4%	20.6%
1% to 9%	100.0%	44.1%	0.6%	31.5%	23.0%	0.7%	76.3%	23.7%
Total	100.0%	40.2%	1.2%	40.2%	17.6%	0.9%	81.5%	18.5%

21

BVR Send questions to: TC-Questions@BVResources.com

© 2010, Business Valuation Resources, LLC

Control Premiums: Applications and Analysis

Control Premium Data – Stock Exchange Statistics

Snapshot of Mergerstat®/BVR Control Premium Database

- There are various stock exchanges tracked by the database. The characteristics of the companies included in each exchange could potentially impact the magnitude of the observed control premiums. Below is an example of premiums under different exchanges in the U.S. and Canada.

Equity Control Premium		
U.S. and Canadian Exchanges		
Exchange	Count	Average
NYSE	873	30.6%
Nasdaq	2,214	37.7%
Amex	203	31.1%
Over-the-Counter	417	47.6%
Toronto	467	32.2%
Canadian Venture	147	61.1%

Invested Capital Control Premium		
U.S. and Canadian Exchanges		
Exchange	Count	Average
NYSE	850	21.1%
Nasdaq	2,150	31.0%
Amex	194	22.2%
Over-the-Counter	410	35.6%
Toronto	439	23.1%
Canadian Venture	134	50.2%

22

BVR Send questions to: TC-Questions@BVResources.com

© 2010, Business Valuation Resources, LLC

Control Premiums: Applications and Analysis

Question: Analyze a Premium to Equity or Invested Capital?

- Three methods are used to apply a control premium:
  1. Unadjusted Equity Premium – calculated or selected equity control premium (percentage) is applied to equity of subject company
  2. Invested Capital or Enterprise Value Premium – calculated or selected control premium (in dollar terms) is divided by invested capital (i.e., entity value) to estimate the control premium (in percentage terms) relative to invested capital.
  3. Adjusted Equity Premium – calculated or selected equity control premium (percentage) is adjusted for differences between the capital structure of the target company and the subject company by scaling the control premium higher (lower) if the target company's equity/total capital level is higher (lower) than the subject company. This method is related to Method 2 discussed above and, assuming consistent data inputs, would result in the same value if used to value the subject company.

23

Send questions to: TC-Questions@BVResources.com

© 2010, Business Valuation Resources, LLC

Control Premiums: Applications and Analysis

Question: Analyze a Premium to Equity or Invested Capital? (Cont.)

- For example, assume that a company with an invested capital value of $100 is acquired for $120, or a 20% control premium to invested capital. Comparing the implications of a 20% control premium to invested capital to the implied control premium to equity over varying debt/capital levels demonstrates the potential for capital structure to significantly impact the equity control premiums reported by Mergerstat® and other databases.

Debt/Capital	Equity Control Premium	Invested Capital Control Premium
0.0%	20.0%	20.0%
5.0%	26.3%	20.0%
10.0%	33.3%	20.0%
15.0%	41.2%	20.0%
20.0%	50.0%	20.0%
25.0%	60.0%	20.0%
30.0%	71.4%	20.0%
35.0%	84.6%	20.0%
40.0%	100.0%	20.0%
45.0%	118.2%	20.0%
50.0%	140.0%	20.0%

24

Send questions to: TC-Questions@BVResources.com

© 2010, Business Valuation Resources, LLC

Control Premiums: Applications and Analysis

Question: Analyze a Premium to Equity or Invested Capital? (Cont.)

- **What does the historical data reported by Mergerstat® indicate?**
  - Compared $ control premiums paid to equity and invested capital
  - Calculate mean and standard deviations of % premiums to equity and invested capital, respectively, based upon different capital structures
  - *Coefficient of variation*, which is measured by dividing standard deviation by mean, is a relative measure of variability and, therefore, is useful for comparing the variability of variables that have different standard deviations and different means.
    - A lower coefficient of variation ("CoV") can be interpreted to mean that the variable under consideration has lower variability or greater consistency than another variable.
  - Measuring dispersion of historical control premiums supports the theoretical notion that benefits of control are based upon factors tied to the value of an entity.
  - For full discussion, see "Control Premiums: Application and Analysis", *Business Valuation Update*, March 2010.

25

BVR Send questions to: TC-Questions@BVResources.com

© 2010, Business Valuation Resources, LLC

Control Premiums: Applications and Analysis

Question: Analyze a Premium to Equity or Invested Capital? (Cont.)

Snapshot of Mergerstat®/BVR Control Premium Database

Table 1

All Industries - All Countries - All Buyers								
Debt / Capital	Count	Equity CP Average	IC CP Average	Equity CP Standard Deviation	IC CP Standard Deviation	Equity CP Coefficient of Variation	IC CP Coefficient of Variation	Equity CoV Lower?
0.0%	946	33.2%	33.1%	57.5%	57.0%	1.73	1.72	No
10.0%	891	30.6%	29.2%	43.2%	39.2%	1.41	1.34	No
20.0%	687	28.1%	24.0%	46.2%	31.1%	1.64	1.30	No
30.0%	523	31.9%	23.9%	39.6%	23.9%	1.24	1.00	No
40.0%	506	32.0%	20.9%	49.1%	20.5%	1.53	0.98	No
50.0%	393	33.3%	18.3%	44.6%	16.8%	1.34	0.92	No
60.0%	303	36.9%	16.7%	60.5%	16.7%	1.64	1.00	No
70.0%	213	42.7%	15.2%	50.2%	10.2%	1.18	0.67	No
80.0%	140	54.4%	13.7%	78.8%	14.9%	1.45	1.08	No
90.0%	108	56.6%	8.6%	73.3%	15.1%	1.29	1.77	Yes
100.0%	63	56.0%	2.9%	52.6%	4.5%	0.94	1.57	Yes

26

BVR Send questions to: TC-Questions@BVResources.com

© 2010, Business Valuation Resources, LLC

Control Premiums: Applications and Analysis

Question: Analyze a Premium to Equity or Invested Capital? (Cont.)

Snapshot of Mergerstat®/BVR Control Premium Database

Table 2

All Industries - U.S. Target Companies Only - All Buyers								
Debt / Capital	Count	Equity CP Average	IC CP Average	Equity CP Standard Deviation	IC CP Standard Deviation	Equity CP Coefficient of Variation	IC CP Coefficient of Variation	Equity CoV Lower?
0.0%	716	36.8%	36.7%	60.2%	59.7%	1.64	1.63	No
10.0%	562	33.0%	31.6%	41.3%	37.2%	1.25	1.18	No
20.0%	404	29.9%	25.5%	44.1%	30.4%	1.48	1.19	No
30.0%	309	34.5%	25.8%	41.3%	24.6%	1.20	0.95	No
40.0%	315	35.4%	23.1%	47.5%	20.1%	1.34	0.87	No
50.0%	247	32.4%	17.9%	42.5%	16.2%	1.31	0.90	No
60.0%	200	37.1%	16.7%	69.1%	16.6%	1.86	0.99	No
70.0%	115	39.5%	14.1%	44.2%	10.1%	1.12	0.71	No
80.0%	92	48.7%	12.4%	93.3%	14.4%	1.92	1.16	No
90.0%	65	63.2%	9.5%	83.4%	16.5%	1.32	1.73	Yes
100.0%	34	96.0%	4.6%	61.1%	5.1%	0.64	1.12	Yes

27

BVR Send questions to: TC-Questions@BVResources.com

© 2010, Business Valuation Resources, LLC

Control Premiums: Applications and Analysis

Question: Analyze a Premium to Equity or Invested Capital? (Cont.)

Snapshot of Mergerstat®/BVR Control Premium Database

Table 3

All Industries - All Countries - Strategic, Vertical, or Horizontal Buyers								
Debt / Capital	Count	Equity CP Average	IC CP Average	Equity CP Standard Deviation	IC CP Standard Deviation	Equity CP Coefficient of Variation	IC CP Coefficient of Variation	Equity CoV Lower?
0.0%	848	33.3%	33.2%	55.3%	55.0%	1.66	1.66	No
10.0%	770	30.3%	28.9%	44.1%	40.1%	1.46	1.39	No
20.0%	593	28.3%	24.1%	46.0%	31.3%	1.63	1.30	No
30.0%	441	33.2%	24.9%	41.9%	25.2%	1.26	1.01	No
40.0%	409	32.2%	21.0%	48.8%	21.0%	1.51	1.00	No
50.0%	313	33.9%	18.7%	45.1%	17.6%	1.33	0.95	No
60.0%	246	37.3%	16.9%	62.5%	17.5%	1.68	1.04	No
70.0%	173	42.9%	15.2%	51.4%	10.5%	1.20	0.69	No
80.0%	109	52.6%	13.1%	81.0%	15.6%	1.54	1.19	No
90.0%	87	59.5%	9.0%	67.2%	15.7%	1.13	1.75	Yes
100.0%	49	43.9%	2.1%	44.1%	3.1%	1.00	1.50	Yes

28

BVR Send questions to: TC-Questions@BVResources.com

© 2010, Business Valuation Resources, LLC

Control Premiums: Applications and Analysis

Question: Analyze a Premium to Equity or Invested Capital? (Cont.)

- **Current Practice**
  - Responses received by The Appraisal Foundation Working Group on Control Premiums from various accounting and valuation firms appears to recognize the theoretical preference for invested capital-based analysis of control premiums.
  - Equity-based control premiums are still most commonly performed in practice. Application of a control premium to equity is acceptable as long as capital structure is considered in the analysis.

29

© 2010, Business Valuation Resources, LLC

Control Premiums in Financial Reporting Engagements

- Despite debate among some valuation specialists about the dubious merits of control premiums, control premiums are often applied when valuing 100% of an entity for financial reporting purposes (for example, when testing goodwill for impairment).
- Emphasis of fair value definition on "exit value" arguably results in more acceptance of synergies being included in a valuation, although theoretically an entity's intrinsic or "stand-alone" value might make more sense for purposes of testing the recoverability of goodwill booked from prior deals.
- However, despite conceptual agreement, significant discussion continues regarding the types and extent of documentation necessary to support a control premium.

30

© 2010, Business Valuation Resources, LLC

Control Premiums in Financial Reporting Engagements (Cont.)

- Much of the focus is on acquisition scenarios that might lead a buyer to pay *more* than current market cap to acquire a company, regardless of whether or not the current stock price includes a minority interest discount.
  - "Substantial value may arise from the ability to take advantage of synergies and other benefits that flow from control over another entity (emphasis added). Consequently, measuring the fair value of a collection of assets and liabilities that operate together in a controlled entity is different from measuring the fair value of that entity's individual equity securities. An acquiring entity often is willing to pay more for equity securities that give it a controlling interest than an investor would pay for a number of equity securities representing less than a controlling interest. That control premium may cause the fair value of a reporting unit to exceed its market capitalization." (Per paragraph 23 of FAS 142 as amended by FAS 157).
- Although the presence of synergies in observed control premium data might invalidate the application of a control premium in certain instances (for example, calculating an implied minority interest discount), the presence of such synergies -if deemed to be market participant synergies- would be acceptable under impairment testing engagements.

31

BVR Send questions to: TC-Questions@BVResources.com

© 2010, Business Valuation Resources, LLC

Control Premiums: Applications and Analysis

Control Premiums in Financial Reporting Engagements: SEC Views

- "If a registrant concludes that their current market capitalization does not reflect fair value then they should understand that the staff may ask them to support the propriety of their control premium or other reasons for such a conclusion. For example, I believe that this support should be based factors such as an evaluation of control premium identifiable in comparable transactions or the cash flows associated with obtaining control of a reporting unit."
- "A percentage selected because it allows the registrant to avoid an impairment or one based on an arbitrary percentage determined by a "rule of thumb" would not appear to be well reasoned…I would also note that the amount of supporting evidence supporting your judgment would likely be expected to increase as any control premium increases."

(Source: Excerpts from December 8, 2008 Speech to the *2008 AICPA National Conference on Current SEC and PCAOB Developments* by Robert G. Fox III, Professional Accounting Fellow, Office of the Chief Accountant of the SEC)

32

BVR Send questions to: TC-Questions@BVResources.com

© 2010, Business Valuation Resources, LLC

Control Premiums: Applications and Analysis

Control Premiums in Financial Reporting Engagements: SEC Views (Cont.)

- "The (SEC) Staff does not have 'bright line' tests that we use in determining the reasonableness of a control premium"
- "Registrants need to carefully analyze the facts and circumstances of their particular situation when determining an appropriate control premium"
- "The amount of supporting evidence supporting a judgment would likely be expected to increase as any control premium increases"

(Source: Excerpts from February 2, 2009 Speech at the *BVR's 2nd Annual Fair Value Summit* by Evan Sussholz, Professional Accounting Fellow – Valuation Specialist, Office of the Chief Accountant of the SEC)

33

BVR Send questions to: TC-Questions@BVResources.com

© 2010, Business Valuation Resources, LLC

Control Premiums: Applications and Analysis

Mark Edwards

- Issues Unique to Control Premiums under Financial Reporting
- Cash Flow-Based Measures of Control Premiums

34

BVR Send questions to: TC-Questions@BVResources.com

© 2010, Business Valuation Resources, LLC

Control Premiums: Applications and Analysis

ASC 350 – Reconciliation

In those engagement where there are multiple reporting units and/or observable market prices of equity:

- The fair value of all reporting units (including those that do not reflect an allocation of goodwill) should be aggregated and tested for overall reasonableness at the consolidated company level.

35

BVR Send questions to: TC-Questions@BVResources.com
© 2010, Business Valuation Resources, LLC
Control Premiums: Applications and Analysis

ASC 350 – Reconciliation for private Companies

1. Estimate the fair value of the entire company on a marketable, controlling basis.

2. Estimate the fair value of all reporting units, including those that do not include an allocation of goodwill, including the "Corporate Unit."
   - In lower risk situations, non-goodwill reporting units may be valued by observed market multiples, implied cap rates or other less extensive techniques.

3. Comparison and reconciliation of the two.

36

BVR Send questions to: TC-Questions@BVResources.com
© 2010, Business Valuation Resources, LLC
Control Premiums: Applications and Analysis

ASC 350 – Reconciliation for public Companies

For purposes of this reconciliation, market capitalization may be calculated as follows:

Shares Outstanding, net of Treasury shares (X)
Share Price (=)
Market Value of Equity

Note: judgment should be used when selecting the time horizon for share price.

37

Send questions to: TC-Questions@BVResources.com

© 2010, Business Valuation Resources, LLC

Control Premiums: Applications and Analysis

ASC 350 – Reconciliation for public companies, continued

Specific reconciling items include the following factors:

1. **Control synergies**
2. **Asymmetric data** -- management may have access to data or information that is not known by the public as of the valuation date
3. **Taxable step-up per ASC 350-20-35** -- difference in taxable and non-taxable
4. **Suboptimal capital structures** -- In some situations, the amount of leverage selected to develop the cost of capital of the market participant is lower than that observed in the public company. A reconciling item can be identified as the difference between discount rates in an optimal and suboptimal capital structure.

38

Send questions to: TC-Questions@BVResources.com

© 2010, Business Valuation Resources, LLC

Control Premiums: Applications and Analysis

Case Study – Facts

Company XYZ

Public company with observable share price of as of the measurement date	$ 3.50
Shares O/S	1,200
Market Cap of Equity	$4,200
Acquirer believes that there are redundant costs that would allow the new company to pick additional 50bp in cost savings. Management believes this savings is permanent	
XYZ is about to launch a new product that will enhance earnings and profits as shown in the DCF used to test for goodwill impairment under ASC 350. All required investment is already reflected on the balance sheet. This information has not been disclosed to the public through filings or press releases	
Non controlling interest of 16.7% outstanding	

39

Send questions to: TC-Questions@BVResources.com

© 2010, Business Valuation Resources, LLC

Control Premiums: Applications and Analysis

Case Study – DCF

XYZ Co.

	2010	2011	2012	2013	2014	Term
Core Revenue	10,000	10,500	10,920	11,248	11,585	11,817
New Product	500	2,000	3,000	3,500	3,800	4,000
Total Revenue	10,500	12,500	13,920	14,748	15,385	15,817
EBITDA - Core	1,200	1,260	1,310	1,350	1,390	1,418
EBITDA - New	75	300	450	525	570	600
Depr/Amtz	30	30	30	30	30	30
Pre Tax Income	1,245	1,530	1,730	1,845	1,930	1,988
Taxes @ 40%	498	612	692	738	772	795
DFNI	747	918	1,038	1,107	1,158	1,193

40

Send questions to: TC-Questions@BVResources.com

© 2010, Business Valuation Resources, LLC

Control Premiums: Applications and Analysis

Case Study – DCF (con't)

XYZ Co.

	2010	2011	2012	2013	2014	Term
CAPX	30	30	30	30	30	30
Depr/Amtz	30	30	30	30	30	30
NWC	125	100	71	41	32	22
DFCF	622	818	967	1,065	1,126	1,171
Periods	0.50	1.50	2.50	3.50	4.50	4.50
PV Factor	0.9366	0.8216	0.7207	0.6322	0.5545	0.5545
Terminal Value 2%						9,760
PV	583	672	697	674	625	5,412
Total FV (Rounde	8,700					
WACC	**14.0%**					
Term Growth	2.0%					

41

Send questions to: TC-Questions@BVResources.com

© 2010, Business Valuation Resources, LLC

Control Premiums: Applications and Analysis

Case Study – Savings

XYZ Co. - Savings to Acquirer

	2010	2011	2012	2013	2014	Term
Core Revenue	10,000	10,500	10,920	11,248	11,585	11,817
New Product Revenue	500	2,000	3,000	3,500	3,800	4,000
Total Revenue	10,500	12,500	13,920	14,748	15,385	15,817
Savings	53	63	70	74	77	79
Taxes @ 40%	21	25	28	29	31	32
DFNI	32	38	42	44	46	47
Periods	0.50	1.50	2.50	3.50	4.50	4.50
PV Factor	0.9206	0.7801	0.6611	0.5603	0.4748	0.4748
Terminal Value 2%						297
PV	29	29	28	25	22	141
Total FV (Rounded)	300					
WACC	**18.0%**					
Term Growth	2.0%					

42

Send questions to: TC-Questions@BVResources.com

© 2010, Business Valuation Resources, LLC

Control Premiums: Applications and Analysis

Case Study – Asymmetric

XYZ Co. - Savings to Acquirer

	2010	2011	2012	2013	2014	Term
New Product Revenue	500	2,000	3,000	3,500	3,800	4,000
Total Revenue	500	2,000	3,000	3,500	3,800	4,000
EBITDA	75	300	450	525	570	600
Taxes @ 40%	30	120	180	210	228	240
DFNI	45	180	270	315	342	360
Periods	0.50	1.50	2.50	3.50	4.50	4.50
PV Factor	0.9206	0.7801	0.6611	0.5603	0.4748	0.4748
Terminal Value 2%						2,250
PV	41	140	179	176	162	1,068
Total FV (Rounded)	1,800					
WACC	**15.0%**					
Term Growth	2.0%					

43

BVR Send questions to: TC-Questions@BVResources.com

© 2010, Business Valuation Resources, LLC

Control Premiums: Applications and Analysis

Case Study – Balance Sheet

XYZ Co
Balance Sheet

Current Assets	2,500	Current Liab (Debt Free)	2,000
PP&E, Net	1,500	Debt	1,500
Intangibles (Finite)	500	NCI	500
Goodwill	2,000	Equity	2,500
Total Assets	6,500		6,500
Carrying Value (Ent)	4,000		

44

BVR Send questions to: TC-Questions@BVResources.com

© 2010, Business Valuation Resources, LLC

Control Premiums: Applications and Analysis

Case Study – Recon

Total Enterprise Fair Value	8,700
Less: Debt	1,500
Implied FV Equity	7,200
Market Cap - Equity	4,200
Implied Premium over Market	71.4%

Market Cap Equity	4,200
Cost Savings	300
Assymetric Impact	1,800
FV of the NCI	756
Total accounted for	7,056
Unexplained	144
% of market Cap	3.4%
% of concluded equity value	2.0%

45

© 2010, Business Valuation Resources, LLC

Andrew Fargason

- Discussion regarding The Appraisal Foundation's Working Group on Control Premiums Best Practices for Financial Reporting

46

© 2010, Business Valuation Resources, LLC

Appraisal Foundation Working Groups

- 3 Current Working Groups, overseen by The Appraisal Foundation's Task Force on Valuations in Financial Reporting (VFR)
  - VFR Working Group 1: Contributory Asset Charges
    - Exposure Drafts issued in 2009
  - VFR Working Group 2: Valuation of Customer-Related Assets
  - VFR Working Group 3: Control Premiums
- Established to develop "best practices" for Valuations in Financial Reporting.
- These Working Groups are developing guidance to assist in reducing diversity in practice in valuations performed for financial reporting purposes.

47

BVR Send questions to: TC-Questions@BVResources.com

© 2010, Business Valuation Resources, LLC

Control Premiums: Applications and Analysis

Control Premium Working Group Update

- VFR Working Group 3: Contributory Asset Charges
  - Includes representatives from accounting firm valuation groups and independent firms
  - Started work in July of 2009
  - Expect to issue exposure draft this year
  - Addressing CP in the Fair Value (accounting) setting only
  - Topics being addressed include:
    - Term definitions
    - Theoretical concepts underlying the issue
    - Best practices for measurement

48

BVR Send questions to: TC-Questions@BVResources.com

© 2010, Business Valuation Resources, LLC

Control Premiums: Applications and Analysis

Control Premium Working Group Update

- VFR Working Group 3: Request for Comments
  - Issued initial Request for Comments Regarding the Assessment and Measurement of Control Premiums in Valuation for Financial Reporting in December.
    - To gather input on a few initial questions
    - Very good response, with some diversity of practice indicated
    - Comment deadline was in January, but the group will still review submissions at this time
    - The Request for Comments can be found on Appraisal Foundation website at:
      - **appraisalfoundation.org (under Financial Reporting)**
    - Includes instructions regarding submission of responses
    - Responses received to date are posted at this same location

49

BVR Send questions to: TC-Questions@BVResources.com

© 2010, Business Valuation Resources, LLC

Control Premiums: Applications and Analysis

Control Premium Working Group Update

- Request for Comments issues include the following topics:

1. Applicability of CP to public market share prices
2. Negative CP
3. Calculation methods – traditional equity method, TIC method
4. Cash flow methods of CP analysis
5. Other methods in use
6. Use of comparable transactions

50

BVR Send questions to: TC-Questions@BVResources.com

© 2010, Business Valuation Resources, LLC

Control Premiums: Applications and Analysis

Q&A

- **Q&A Session**

51

BVR Send questions to: TC-Questions@BVResources.com

© 2010, Business Valuation Resources, LLC

Control Premiums: Applications and Analysis

Control Premiums: Applications and Analysis

BVR
What It's Worth

Business Valuation Resources, LLC
(888) 287-8258 or (503) 291-7963
www.BVResources.com

Brad Pursel
CPA/ABV, CFA, ASA | Brown Smith Wallace LLC
Mark Edwards
CPA/ABV, CFA | Grant Thornton, LLP
Andrew Fargason
CFA | American Appraisal

BVR © 2010, Business Valuation Resources, LLC

Send questions to: TC-Questions@BVResources.com

Court Case Abstracts

ASARCO v. Americas Mining Corp.

Case Considers Control Premiums, DCF Discount Rates, and More

Citation: 2008 WL 4009927(S.D. Tex.)
Date of decision: Aug. 30, 2008
Country: US
State/Jurisdiction: Texas
Court: United States District Court
Type of action: Bankruptcy
Experts: Navigant (plaintiff/debtor); Craig Pirrong (defendant)
Judge: Hanen
SIC: 1021 -- Specific categories --

By 2003, a century-old mining company had entered "the zone of insolvency," according to its valuation and legal advisors. Its most valuable asset: a 54% controlling interest in a Peruvian copper concern, which was worth between $600 million and nearly $1 billion. When its parent company decided to purchase the asset, those same advisors warned the board of directors that it would be difficult to justify the transaction "consistent with its fiduciary duty to protect all creditors" of the subsidiary. But the directors pressed forward with the sale, and the troubled subsidiary struggled for nearly two more years. In 2005 it declared bankruptcy, and as Chapter 11 debtor, it tried to recoup the sale of its "crown jewel" as a fraudulent transfer.

Valuation experts parse elements of purchase. In its 107-page opinion, the federal district court first examined the debtor's claims for constructive fraud—in particular, whether the debtor received "reasonably equivalent value" in exchange for its controlling interest in the Peruvian copper company. (The debtor also claimed actual fraud, which required a showing of actual intent to hinder or delay creditors.)

Both parties agreed that the parent company paid $765 million, composed of: 1) $450 million cash, used to pay down the debtor's revolving line of credit; 2) $50 million, to pay down "Yankee bonds" ($100 million of outstanding, unsecured bonds); 3) a promissory note payable for $123.25 million; 4) a guarantied promissory note for $100 million; and 5) a cancellation of $41.75 million in debt.

The debtor's expert concluded that the consideration was worth between $660.2 million and $726.6 million—prior to subtracting the negative, net economic effects of paying off the Yankee bonds, which reduced the value to between $611.2 million and $702.11 million. By contrast, the expert for the parent company valued the consideration at $720.3 million—without any reduction for the bond payoff. The court examined each element:

1. Cash. The parties—and the court—agreed that the $450 million cash paid to retire the revolving debt was worth $450 million.

2. Yankee bonds. The parent company claimed that the $50 million payoff of the Yankee bonds was worth $50 million to the subsidiary/debtor. The debtor's expert argued that because the bonds were trading below par, the court should discount their net economic benefit to the debtor. But the court held that the trading discount did not reduce the value of $50 million cash, and credited the consideration accordingly.

3. $123.5 million note. The parent owed seven annual installments of $17.6 million to pay off the principal of the note. The debtor's expert estimated its present value between $78.6 million and $105.7 million; this essentially conformed to an analysis by Ernst & Young (E&Y), the debtor's advisors during the sale, which used a discount rate between 12.5% and 25%. The parent's expert used varying discount rates, however, ranging from 17.55% to 19.36%, based on a credit spread of 16.43%; he valued the note at $94.36 million. The court found this approach more reasonable, "somewhat buoyed by the fact that it falls within the center of the ranges found by [the debtor's experts]."

4. $100 million note. The debtor's expert relied on the E&Y analysis, which applied lower discount rates—10% to 12.5%, because the parent guaranteed the eight installments payments of $12.5 million, resulting in a present value for the note of $85.1 million to $91.4 million. The expert for the parent company examined its credit rating and prevailing market yields, determined a spread of 4.55% and discount rates of 5.68% to 7.99%, and valued the note at $99.8 million. But the court found his rates too low, and valued the note at the higher end of the debtor's range, or $91.2 million. (The court didn't explain its reasoning—but its value falls almost midway between the experts'.)

5. Debt forgiveness. The parent company cancelled a $41.75 million past-due note from the subsidiary; its expert valued this debt forgiveness at $26.12, based on a renegotiation of the debt at 9.28% interest over an extended term. The debtor's expert claimed the value was worth up to 100% of the debt—and the court agreed, finding the situation analogous to the payment of the Yankee bonds. It was not appropriate to reduce the value of the debt cancellation based on the "mere possibility" of a renegotiation, it said, and valued this element at $475 million.

Overall, the court found that the debtor received $727.8 million in exchange for its stake in the Peruvian mining company. The next question became the value of this 54% controlling interest.

Public markets not always the most reliable measure. In addition to valuations by the parties' experts, the court considered the E&Y appraisals plus ones by Behre Dolbear and Houlihan Lokey (Houlihan), all conducted at the time of the sale. Each appraisal applied the three commonly accepted approaches for valuing publicly traded stock: 1) stock price valuation; 2) market multiples; and 3) discounted cash flow (DCF). In this case, the 54% interest was comprised of "Founders Shares" with enhanced voting rights. Additional founders owned enhanced shares (five votes per share) but all were thinly traded, less than 1% active in the open market.

The parent's expert believed that the stock's price on the day of sale was the best indicator of value, given the efficiencies of a "semi-strong" market, which factored in elements of control. But the debtor's expert did not believe the market for the Peruvian mining company was efficient, especially given a "serendipitously low" stock price on the day of sale. The debtor's expert also advocated a control premium.

Relying on Delaware law, the court recognized that the market price "may not always" represent the true value of publicly traded shares. And pursuant to a leading federal case (*Cammer v. Bloom*, D. N.J., 1989), it examined the Peruvian stock under several criteria, including average weekly trading volume, the number of securities analysts following the stock, and the company's public filings. At the time of the transfer, the stock was traded on the "extremely reliable" New York Stock Exchange—but its low trading volume and thin public float cut against the presumptive market efficiencies.

The debtor contended that a 20-, 30-, or 60- day trailing price would be more appropriate. "Mainstream valuation" practice used this approach to smooth out stock volatilities, their expert said. In fact, Ernst & Young had used a 60-day trailing average in addition to a single-day price in its analysis, and Houlihan used a 20-day trailing average of stock prices. Moreover, the stock on the day of sale reached its lowest price—$14.60 per share, compared to $15.00 and $16.00 per share in prior months. The court agreed with this approach, finding the stock sufficiently volatile to warrant using a trailing average, especially since the number of days selected resulted in similar pricing for the debtor's interest: $671 million for a 20-day average; $676 million over 30-days; and $678.8 million over sixty.

Market price accounts for control? The debtor's urged the court to apply a 30% to 40% control premium to the 54% Founders' stake. Houlihan had applied a 20% premium in its analysis, and E&Y had applied a 30% premium in its market approach. (Because investors knew the stock was "in play," E&Y did not apply a control premium in its stock valuation.) The debtor's expert adopted a 30% premium, based on 2002 Mergerstat data that showed 12-month median and average control premia in the mining industry of 25.9% and 39.5%, respectively.

The parent company argued that no premium was appropriate. Not only did the market price factor in control, but an independent, third party buyer could lose the enhanced voting rights associated with the 54% interest if the remaining founders acquired enough enhanced shares, with five-votes-per, to effectively obtain a controlling interest. Further, the Mergerstat data overvalued control because it did not consider synergies or account for negative premiums. If any premium was appropriate, it should be only 7% or 8%.

But the court found this range too low. A third-party buyer would pay a premium for the 54% controlling block, it said, despite the risk of the remaining founders buying a controlling share—which was "relatively low," given their lack of desire, means, or notice. Any distinction between synergies and control was misplaced, because a buyer wouldn't "mechanically" separate the reasons for paying a premium, the court said. But a 30% premium was too high; E&Y had only used this in its market approach, and the debtor failed to convince the court that Mergerstat data should be added directly to the market price. Overall, the 20% control premium that Houlihan used in its contemporaneous analysis of the sale (and in a prior fairness opinion) was the more reasonable, the court said. Applying this to a 30-day trailing average, it valued the debtor's 54% interest under the stock valuation approach at $811.4 million.

Company-specific risk is key to market approach. The expert for the parent company rejected any guideline public company analysis, claiming that it was "highly unreliable as a standalone methodology," particularly if the information to conduct a "full-blown" DCF is available and the comparable mining companies weren't sufficiently similar to the Peruvian concern. However, the court noted that the expert had used market multiples in his DCF determination of terminal value; it also believed that a willing buyer would consider the market approach as a "sanity check" against a DCF and stock valuation. Moreover, the remaining experts had used the comparable company approach, as follows:

1. After selecting five copper and mining companies, E&Y determined the debtor's interest in the Peruvian company was worth $644 million. To account for specific-company risk, it adjusted this amount downward by 30%, then applied the 30% control premium.

2. Houlihan used five of the same comparables plus an additional three, but did not include the downward adjustment before adding a 20% control premium.

3. Behre Dolbear used market multiples of EBITDA, and averaged its results with those from its comparable transactions and DCF analyses, before adding a 25% control premium without any downward adjustment.

4. The debtor's expert adopted the E&Y analysis, without the 30% downward adjustment.

5. In his DCF analysis, the expert for the parent company did not adjust his market multiples for a control premium or company-specific risk.

The experts also debated the mining risks in Peru—the debtor's believed the risks were low to moderate, while the expert for the parent company claimed that they were higher than those in any of the top twelve copper-producing countries during the relevant time period. Setting these arguments aside, the court didn't see sufficient objective evidence for applying the 30% downward adjustment. The comparable companies captured the risks in their betas and other numbers, and any further assessment seemed "arbitrary and speculative."

But the company numbers did not account for control. Relying on its stock price analysis, the court found an appropriate control premium to range between 20% and 30%. Using the equity that E&Y derived in its comparable companies approach, minus the downward adjustment, the court found the debtor's interest to be worth $890 million (20% control premium), $928 million (25%), and $965 (30%). It briefly considered the comparable transactions approach, but concluded (with most of the experts) that the available datasets were neither helpful nor reliable.

DCF turns first on copper prices. The court also agreed with the experts that in this case, the DCF was the most reliable method for valuing the debtor's holdings in the Peruvian copper concern. The critical variables were the price of copper and the correct discount rate.

To determine the first, the court considered the prices used by valuation analysts at the time of the sale (2003), along with contemporaneous price forecasts by industry and financial analysts, the company's internal forecasts, and evidence from the trial experts. For instance, Behre Dolbear looked at 15-year forecasts that projected an average price of $0.96 per pound and concluded that the industry expected long-term prices to range between $0.90 and $0.95 per pound. It used three different prices ($0.85, $0.90, and $0.96) to conduct three different DCFs, and considered the range of $0.90 to $0.92 per-pound to be appropriate.

The debtor's expert looked at price forecasts from 2003 to 2007, and calculated the average of the median to be $0.95 cents. During the relevant time period, the debtor was using a range of $0.90 to $0.92 for their internal forecasts, including a ten-year average of $0.91. In their 2001 and 2002 10-ks, the debtor used $0.90 to value its copper reserves and long-term prices. Accordingly, the debtor's expert used $0.90 and $0.95 in its DCF analyses.

By contrast, Houlihan used a price of $0.85 per pound in its analysis at the time of the sale, but ultimately the court was convinced that $0.90 was the appropriate long-term price for copper, "especially as that was the price used internally by [the debtor.]"

Discount rates stir *Daubert* debate. "One of the most hard fought aspects of this trial was which discount rate should be applied and how it should be calculated," the court said, prompting the parties to file "dueling *Daubert* motions." (It dismissed both motions, saying the experts' use of different methods, Fama-French versus the capital asset pricing model (CAPM), went to the weight and not the admissibility of the evidence.)

Only the parent company's expert used the Fama-French method to calculate a discount rate of 13.4%. The remaining experts used CAPM to calculate discount rates that ranged from 9% (E&Y) to 10% (Houlihan). The Fama-French approach was primarily used by academics and resulted in a rate outside the range of the CAPM calculations, the court said. It found that a discount rate between 9% and 10% "would not be unreasonable," but that the 9% rate used by the debtor's expert and E&Y was "most appropriate" in valuing the debtor's interest.

After reviewing the expert's various DCF models, the court also decided that the debtor's expert presented the "most accurate model." Using this model and the 9% discount rate, and inputting the long-term copper price of $0.90, the court found the value of the debtor's interest to be $853 million. (The court also applied discount rates of 9.5% and 10%, and found resulting values of $775.3 and $708.3 million, respectively.)

The bottom line on reasonably equivalent value. To sum up the court's value determinations:

- Stock price approach: $811.4 million (30-day trailing average and 20% control premium)
- Market (comparable company) approach: $890 million (20% control premium, no company-specific risk premium)
- DCF (income) approach: $853 million (9% discount rate, $0.90 long-term copper price)

The court found the result of the comparable company analysis to be outside the range of the other two methods, and agreed with the majority of experts who used it only as a reasonableness check. It concluded that the debtor's 54% stake in the Peruvian copper company was worth between $811.4 million and $ 853 million. Contrasting this against the debtor's receipt of $727.8 million from the parent, the court found the difference "not insubstantial." However, "percentage-wise," the numbers looked much closer: The consideration comprised approximately 85% to 90% of the value transferred, "well above the 70% rule" articulated by leading cases on reasonably equivalent value.

The court also considered the totality of circumstances surrounding the transaction. Although it lacked independence and arms-length, at the time of the sale, copper prices were only $0.71 per pound. In addition, the debtor's financial advisors (E&Y) provided an opinion that the sale was financially fair. "The law does not demand that a plaintiff receive an amount equal to the fair market value of the asset it transfers," the court said, "the consideration must only be *reasonably* equivalent." Given all the facts of the case, including "the lack of precision" inherent in valuing the mining company stock, the court found that the debtor received reasonable value in exchange for its stake.

Parent, directors still face liability. In the second half of its lengthy opinion, the court considered the debtor's claims of actual fraud and found that the parent company "entered into the...transaction with the full knowledge that [the debtor's] creditors would be hindered or delayed as a result." It also found that the debtor was insolvent at the time of the transfer. Although the directors of the parent did not beach any direct fiduciary duties, they "aided and abetted" the subsidiary's directors by structuring the deal to deprive the "cash-starved" debtor of is most valuable asset. (Many of the directors sat on both boards.) The court denied the debtor's claims for punitive damages, but given its favorable rulings on actual fraud and aiding/abetting, it directed the parties to address damages in further briefs.

The court also noted that the parties had already spent "millions of dollars" on the case, including fees for over thirty attorneys and experts. In an unusual step, it made additional, alternate findings on key rulings, anticipating review by the Fifth Circuit court in an almost certain appeal.

Stuart Agranoff, et al. v. Edward M. Miller, et al.

Fair Market Value and Fair Value Determined

Date of decision: 5/15/2001
Country: US
State or Federal: State
State/Jurisdiction: Delaware
Court: Court of Chancery
Type of action: Miscellaneous

In *Stuart Agranoff, et al. v. Edward M. Miller, et al.*, No. 16795 (May 15, 2001), the Delaware Court of Chancery determined the value of warrants improperly purchased by Miller. Miller and the plaintiffs were shareholders in EMS, a company holding 62 percent of an express delivery and courier business. Bankers Trust (BT) held warrants to 35.284 percent of EMS's stock on a fully diluted basis. The warrants were exercisable for $1 per share. The warrants as well as the issued common stock were subject to plaintiffs' right of first refusal. Miller engaged in a conspiracy to achieve control of EMS. As part of his conspiracy, he induced BT and some of the minority shareholders to sell their stock to him without first offering it to the plaintiffs. He purchased the minority shareholders' stock (those holding less than 15 percent) for less than $30 per share, while he paid $60.37 per share for the warrants. Thereafter, the plaintiffs brought suit against Miller for usurpation of corporate opportunity, among other claims.

After successive appeals and appearances before the Delaware Supreme Court, it concluded that the plaintiffs had the right to purchase the warrants wrongfully acquired by Miller for the lesser of Miller's purchase price or the price the plaintiffs could have obtained for the warrants. It further stated, "That hypothetical purchase price, which we assume will be a 'fair value' price equivalent to that determined through appraisal, is a factual determination, which must be made by the Court of Chancery." In reaching its decision regarding the measure of damages in this case, the Supreme Court noted that the price Miller paid to acquire the warrants included a control premium, which the stock would not have commanded had the purchaser been one of the plaintiffs.

Before the Court of Chancery, the parties argued over the proper interpretation of the Supreme Court's order. Miller argued that a literal reading of the Supreme Court's order required that the hypothetical purchase price be the fair value of the stock (i.e. a valuation of the stock as a going concern absent discounts for lack of marketability or minority interest). Agranoff argued that Miller's interpretation contradicted the spirit of the Supreme Court's order. He argued that the hypothetical purchase price should be the fair market value of the stock. The Court of Chancery agreed with Agranoff that a fair value determination would contradict the Supreme Court's comment regarding a control premium. However, since it found that both parties' arguments had merit in light of the order's ambiguity, the Court of Chancery valued the stock under both standards of value.

Both parties presented expert testimony regarding the value of the stock. The plaintiffs' valuation expert calculated the value of the business using the discounted cash flow (DCF) method. He adjusted the company's projections after discussions with the company's managers. The Court of Chancery found it possible that hindsight bias could have infected his projection adjustments. It further stated, "[Plaintiffs'] DCF analysis seems like an unreliable way to have those actual [post valuation date] results influence the court's valuation in an indirect manner that is not susceptible to fair evaluation. Nor have the plaintiffs provided finance literature supporting the acceptance of [this]... approach to projection modification." The court further noted that the plaintiffs' valuation focused on equity rather than entity value, which did not consider different capital structures of corporations. Thus, it rejected this expert's valuation.

Miller's expert considered a discounted cash flow valuation but declined to value the business under that method because the company's projections were unreliable on the valuation date. He valued the stock using three comparable public company analyses-revenue analysis, earnings before interest and taxes (EBIT), and earnings before interest, taxes, depreciation and amortization (EBITDA). He used three comparable companies to derive his multiples and adjusted for size and lack of marketability. He adjusted the multiple applied to revenue upward from the median indicated by the comparables due to EMS's short-term business plan and sales. He adjusted the EBIT and EBITDA multiples downward because of EMS's poor profit margin.

The court accepted this valuation with one adjustment. It agreed with the plaintiffs' that an upward adjustment to the revenue multiple was inappropriate. It found this expert's revenue multiple too optimistic in light of the fact that the company consistently failed to meet its EBITDA targets. The court further found the revenue multiple inconsistent with the expert's EBIT and EBITDA multiples. After making the adjustment to the revenue multiple, the court equally weighted the results of the three comparable company analyses and determined that EMS had a marketable minority value of $41.02 per share. It then considered the discounts or premiums each party applied to determine the fair market value. Miller argued for a control premium of 20 percent to apply because the warrants represented a large block guaranteeing control to the plaintiff purchasers, thus, warranting an upward adjustment. The plaintiffs lobbied for a 33 percent lack of marketability discount. The Court of Chancery declined to apply either a control premium or a lack of marketability discount, reasoning that the two adjustments roughly cancelled each other out after considering the voting power represented by the warrants.

The court then considered the appropriate control premium to apply to the fair market value in order to determine the fair value of the company. The court noted that the evidence of control premiums includes amounts paid by acquirers for transactionally-specific factors such as synergy, and does not indicate a 'pure' control premium paid by a purchaser when nothing changes but the identity of the majority stockholder. It further noted that transactionally specific factors may not be considered in the calculation of the control premium for appraisal purposes. It noted, "For this very reason, the cases in which this court has adjusted minority discounts to exclude value that derives from the expectation of a synergistic change in control have used a necessarily rough approach that simply involves shaving some percentage off the top of the available information about control premiums paid." It then considered the experts' opinions. Miller's expert argued that a 40 percent control premium was appropriate. This was based on control premiums paid during acquisitions of publicly traded companies in 1998. The plaintiffs' argue that 1998 was a year for mega-mergers, which were not comparable to the subject company. They also pointed out that two delivery service industry companies were acquired that year. The premiums paid in those acquisitions were only 16.7 percent. The Court of Chancery then concluded that a 30 percent control premium should be applied in order to determine the fair value of the shares. The court noted that this premium reflected the fact that the subject company was not comparable to the companies acquired in 1998, the reduced premium paid in acquisitions of delivery companies in 1998, and a reduction for transaction-specific factors. It concluded that the fair value of the stock was $51.13 per share.

Kathryn Casey v. Amboy Bancorporation

New Jersey Considers Fair Value and Synergy

Date of decision: 8/8/2006
Country: US
State or Federal: State
State/Jurisdiction: New Jersey
Court: Court of Appeals
Type of action: Dissenting Shareholder

In *Kathryn Casey v. Amboy Bancorporation*, No. A-0715-04T3 (N.J. Supr. August 8, 2006), the New Jersey Superior Court, Appellate Division considered a lower court's calculation of fair value and its treatment of synergies in this dissenters' rights action. In 1997, Amboy Bancorporation, a C corporation, sought to convert to an S corporation. Since an S corporation was limited to 75 shareholders and Amboy had in excess of 400 shareholders, it determined to execute a cash-out merger that eliminated shareholders having less than 15,000 shares. The cash-out price was determined to be $73 per share, which was supported by a fairness opinion. Several suits were spawned from this transaction. The fair value issues were consolidated into one action, which has been to the appellate division twice before.

The lower court determined the fair value of the stock in the second remand. Five experts, including one appointed by the court, testified to the fair value of the stock. The court noted that fair value was defined as the going concern value, exclusive of appreciation or depreciation resulting from the contested event and exclusive of discounts for minority interest or lack of marketability. However, the court found that a control premium may be warranted, but in considering a control premium care should be taken to exclude a synergistic value arising from the contested transaction.

The company's expert sought to value the bank on the basis of comparable stock for cash transactions because the operative reality of the transaction was stock-for-cash. In doing so, he removed excess capital from the valuation since minority shareholders could not access the capital. The trial court rejected reliance upon stock-for-cash transactions because the operative reality was that 90% of bank transactions were acquisition transactions involving stock-for-stock swaps.

It rejected one dissenter's appraiser, who valued the business based on the comparable public company method and the discounted cash flow (DCF) method. It found that this expert utilized too high a discount rate in his DCF method and dissimilar comparables. Additionally, it found that this expert took each opportunity to issue an updated report as an opportunity to increase the value of the subject company's stock.

The court preferred the approach of an expert that valued the business based on comparable acquisitions, which included embedded control premiums. His valuation resulted in $120 per share. While he acknowledged that synergy value was generally included in control premiums, there was no method to extract the synergistic premium from the overall control premium. Moreover, he tested his valuation using a proprietary feasibility analysis, which was fully explained at trial. Under this analysis, he identified seven potential acquirers and concluded that only two could undertake an acquisition of the subject company at $120 per share without diluting their own earnings, but six companies could undertake the acquisition at a price of $114 per share.

The court rejected the court appointed expert's public company guideline method. The court found it problematic to value the business on a marketable minority basis and apply a control premium. The expert reasoned that some synergistic value may be imbedded in the marketable minority per share price, thus double counting the synergistic value in the control premium, if the market believed that the subject company was to be imminently acquired. However, the court credited this expert's opinion that 90% of the transactions were consummated using stock-for-stock transactions. Moreover, he testified that synergistic value represented between 3 and 5% of a transaction price.

It rejected another expert because he utilized incomparable companies in his analysis, failed to make a feasibility analysis, and declined to address the issue of synergy.

The court adopted the $114 per share value. It determined that this was the highest feasible sale price of the stock. Several parties appealed.

The parties' appeals break down into two complaints: (1) the trial court erred when it valued the stock at fair value using the highest feasible sale price, and (2) the trial court improperly accounted for the effects of synergy. The appellate court disagreed on both counts.

On the first point, the appellate division noted that New Jersey's fair value statute is similar to Delaware's, and New Jersey courts appropriately look to both Delaware law and the American Law Institute for guidance on appraisal issues because they agree that the main objective of appraisal statues is the protection of the minority shareholder. In making this pronouncement the court stated, "That means a court may rely on the provision in 2 ALI Principles, supra, § 7.22(c), that courts 'generally should give substantial weight to the highest realistic price that a willing, able, and fully informed buyer would pay for the corporation as an entity.'" It further noted that the trial judge is limited in his selection of valuation methods to only those that are "legally acceptable" and "reasonable."

Amboy Corporation argued that the trial court erred when it utilized comparable stock-for-stock transactions rather than stock-for-cash transactions since the operative reality of the underlying transaction was stock-for-cash. The appellate court rejected this argument. It noted that the testimony showed that when valuing an acquisition target, the market reality was that 90% of transactions were stock-for-stock transactions. Moreover, it noted that Delaware case law supports the position that stock-for-stock transactions provide an adequate basis for computing going concern value. Therefore, it affirmed the lower court's decision to value the business as a going concern by reference to stock-for-stock transactions.

Amboy further argued that the trial court erred when it relied upon the expert's proprietary feasibility study in determining the fair value of the stock because that proprietary method was not generally accepted in the appraisal community. The appellate court rejected this argument. It reasoned that since the "feasibility analysis was a confirmatory test separate from the acquisition valuation itself, [the trial judge] ... did not err by finding it credible for its stated purpose without concern for whether its methodology was generally accepted as a primary valuation tool." It further stated, "Our courts have readily recognized that valuation, which relies on significant exercises of judgment, is accordingly more of an art than a science; that makes it only natural for experts to use different 'proprietary' approaches rather than a rigidly uniform methodology, and for the trial court to assess their credibility and decide for itself how much reliance they merit when determining fair value in the particular circumstances before it."

Amboy lastly argued that the trial court's use of stock-for-stock transactions as an indictor of fair value violated its federal right to reorganize itself as an S corporation. The appellate division rejected this position, finding that "Amboy seeks to elevate its desires to maintain Amboy's independence above its duty to pay fair value as defined by statute and case law." Since there was no authority presented for that position, the court concluded that Amboy had an obligation to pay its shareholders fair value, and if it could not do so, it needed to find an alternative.

The court then considered the second prong of the arguments: those relating to synergy.

One question presented to the court by the parties was whether the trial court erred when it reduced the going concern value of the business for inherent synergies arising from the conversion of the company from a C corporation to an S corporation. The experts agreed that control premiums were present in comparable stock-for-stock acquisitions, but that any value allocated to synergies could not be quantified. Nonetheless, the experts opined that synergies could make up as much as 5% of the value of the stock or $5 per share on $120 per share.

The trial court was required to adhere to the fair value statute and the remand instructions. They required that the subject company be valued without depreciation or appreciation arising from the contested action, but that a control premium should be applied so long as it did not include any synergistic value. Furthermore, the court could adjust the values in order to comply with this mandate. The trial court did just that. It valued the business based on comparable stock-for-stock transactions that included control premiums. It received evidence regarding the value allocated to synergies. While acknowledging that there was no reliable estimate of the embedded synergies in a control premium, it estimated a $6 dollar adjustment from the value computed by reference to comparable transactions. The parties appealed this adjustment.

On appeal, the parties argued that the trial court erroneously adjusted for the synergies by adjusting for synergies in the comparable transactions when the fair value statute required only exclusion of synergies arising from the contested transaction. The appellate court noted:

> [The trial judge] correctly observed that the synergies embedded in the prices at which comparable mergers occurred did not cease to exist simply because outsiders could not have as clear a view of them as the participants, and furthermore, that applying the financial multiples derived from those prices without a synergy adjustment necessarily carried the synergy element into the resulting valuation .... His determination that the acquisition valuations needed a synergy adjustment was logically unavoidable, and consistent with our categorical instruction to exclude synergies.

Moreover, in the absence of direct evidence of the quantum of synergistic value, the trial court did not err in estimating the effect of this transaction's synergistic value. The court noted that this approach is in accordance with Delaware law. In Delaware, the courts have adjusted for the synergistic element by (1) adjusting the prices of comparable transactions based on expert testimony as to the effect of synergy on value, or (2) they "consider the simple existence of a range of otherwise legally acceptable valuations as a demonstration that synergies are present." Since the trial court valued the business based on the highest feasible price, it was appropriate to apply a discount to back out the synergies. The judge relied upon the testimony of three experts, which included a feasibility analysis, an opinion that the $5 of a $120 per share price was synergy, and an opinion that 5% was a reasonable general estimate for synergies. Since the trial judge's analysis was supported by the record and comparable to analyses applied in Delaware, the appellate court affirmed the synergy deduction.

Cede & Co. v. JRC Acquisition Corp., et al.

Fair Value of Tobacco Retailer Determined

Date of decision: 2/4/2004
Country: US
State or Federal: State
State/Jurisdiction: Delaware
Court: Court of Chancery
Type of action: Dissenting Shareholder

In *Cede & Co. v. JRC Acquisition Corp., et al.*, No. 18648-NC (Del. Chan. February 10, 2004), the Delaware Court of Chancery determined the fair value of 652,400 shares of 800-JR Cigar, Inc. (JR Cigar). JR Cigar was a publicly traded company in the retail cigar and tobacco industry. The Rothman family collectively held 78 percent of its stock, and sought to take the company private. By late September 2000, the Rothman family had acquired more than 90 percent of JR Cigar's stock. On October 4, 2000 JR Cigar effected a short form merger, which cashed out the remaining interests in it for $13 per share. Merrill Lynch issued a fairness opinion in connection with the merger. It considered the value of JR Cigar under the comparable transaction method, which indicated a value of $12 per share, and the discounted cash flow method, which indicated a value between $9.49 and $12.63 per share. Cede dissented to the transaction and sought judicial appraisal of its interest. Both parties presented expert testimony regarding the fair value of JR Cigar to the Chancery Court.

Cede's expert was a credentialed business appraiser. He valued JR Cigar using two methods: the comparable transaction and discounted cash flow methods. Cede's expert considered the transaction used by Merrill Lynch in its fairness opinion. However, Cede's expert determined a different transaction was "most comparable." He adjusted the transaction to account for fluctuations in the market between the announcement of the transaction and its consummation. On cross-examination, the expert conceded that the transaction differentiated in several respects from the dissented-to-transaction: (1) the dissented-to-transaction was a going private transaction while the transaction used by the expert was a synergistic merger, and (2) the transaction at issue involved a tobacco retailer while the transaction used by the expert involved a tobacco product manufacturer. The court rejected this expert's comparable transaction valuation. It stated, "Most of these errors were exposed on cross examination, as he [Cede's expert] was unable to fully defend his methodology. Witnessing ... [Cede's expert]'s testimony first-hand convinces me once again that 'no substitute has ever been found for cross-examination as a means of ... reducing exaggerated statements to their true dimensions.'"

The company's expert, a professor of economics, also used several methods to value the business, including two market approaches. His first market approach measured control premiums. He considered 2,077 transactions between 1995 and 2000. He limited that universe to transactions where the purchaser held at least 75 percent of the company. The remaining 31 transactions had a median control premium of 17 percent, which was less than the 21 percent indicated by the dissented-to-transaction. Cede argued that this approach "violated the concept of comparability." The Chancery Court agreed because the universe of transactions was not sorted by industry or date and the underlying data had a standard deviation of 32 percent. Moreover, it stated, "Additionally, it is not clear that any analysis of premiums over all transactions has any bearing on 'fair value' in an appraisal action, even if it may bear on how efficiencies arising from a merger could equitably be apportioned between buyers and sellers." Thus, it rejected this methodology.

The company's expert also considered the "market check" performed by the company's financial advisors. The advisors shopped JR Cigar prior to the dissented-to-transaction to two potential purchasers. Neither expressed interest. The expert found this evidence persuasive of the fact that the merger consideration was greater than what any potential acquirer was willing to pay. The court rejected this argument. It stated, "Little can be drawn from the fact these two buyers declined to make an offer. Additionally, simply because no rival bidders appeared after the announcement of the going private proposal does not help the Court ascertain the fair value of JR Cigar."

The court lastly considered both experts' discounted cash flow valuations. The experts used the capital asset pricing model (CAPM) to determine the cost of equity for using in their weighted average cost of capital (WACC). The experts' valuations differed in four respects: (1) the estimated growth rate in perpetuity, (2) the appropriate debt-to-equity ratio, (3) the appropriate equity size premium, and (4) the appropriate tax rate.

The court first considered the appropriate growth rate. The company's expert utilized 2.5 to 3.5 percent, which equaled or exceeded the rate of long-term inflation. Cede's expert utilized 5 percent, based on long-term projections prepared by JR Cigar's lender. The court rejected Cede's attempt to classify the document as a management projection; it determined that the document was the lender's extrapolation of management's five-year projections. It then considered the possibility of JR Cigar's growth through the elimination of its competitors and the overall decline in the tobacco products market. Based on that evidence, it determined that the appropriate growth rate was 3.5 percent, which it found accounted for the possibility of growth in a declining market.

The court next considered the appropriate debt-to-equity ratio. The company's expert utilized a 10 percent debt-to-equity ratio. In selecting this ratio, he noted that the company carried no debt, the only other publicly held tobacco retailer also carried no debt, and JR Cigar's management did not anticipate taking on any substantial debt. Cede's expert used a 25 percent debt-to-equity ratio. In arriving at that figure, he considered that JR Cigar carried 17 percent debt-to-equity prior to its 1997 IPO, comparable companies had similar ratios, and the company's expansion opportunities required it to take on additional debt. It lastly noted that the company took on $55 million in debt to consummate the cash out merger The Chancery Court rejected Cede's expert's opinion. It found that the consideration of the pre-IPO debt-to-equity ratio was inappropriate because it was temporally distant and the proceeds of the IPO were used to pay down its debt. Moreover, the comparables considered by the expert were not comparable because they were manufacturers rather than retailers. It lastly found that no evidence suggested that JR Cigar would have to take on a substantial amount of debt to expand, when it had over $13 million in cash and equivalents. The court lastly rejected Cede's evidence that the company took on debt as a result of the dissented-toevent. It noted, "Petitioner's consideration of such debt contravenes the valuation statute's command to appraise shares 'exclusive of any element of arising from the accomplishment or expectation of the merger.'" Thus, the Chancery Court accepted the opinion of the company's expert on this issue.

The Chancery Court then turned to the equity size premium issue. Both experts used data from *Ibbottson* to arrive at their premium. The company's expert selected the premium (2.6 percent) from the micro-cap category; he reasoned that based on the trading price of the stock before the announcement of the merger, the company had a market capitalization below $192 million. Cede's expert selected the premium (1.1 percent) from the low-cap category. He reasoned that the stock price of JR Cigar was depressed; therefore, he determined the fair value implied market capitalization. The company's expert argued that Cede's methodology was "somewhat circular because the whole purpose of the DCF analysis is to ascertain JR Cigar's fair value." Moreover, he argued that "*Ibottson* data already incorporates illiquidity and depressed values since it is derived exclusively from traded stock prices." The court stated, " Regardless of whether or not adjusting the equity size premium based on implied fair value is appropriate in some circumstances, I ultimately determine that the record in this case does not support ... [Cede's] methodology." It agreed that the stock was depressed because of the small amount of public shares, its small market capitalization, and the decline in the tobacco industry. It noted, "The failure to isolate the specific impact of JR Cigar's illiquidity on its stock price undermines Petitioner's analysis." It further reasoned, "The problem with using liquidity as a basis for justifying a lower expected return, however, is that low liquidity is associated with higher expected returns. Investors seek compensation for high transaction costs of illiquid securities, e.g., the bid/ask spread. In other words, even if JR Cigar had a higher market capitalization than the market price of its stock suggested *because of its illiquidity*, investors would still expect higher returns *because of its illiquidity*." (Emphasis in original). Thus, the Court utilized the micro-cap premium.

The court lastly considered the tax rate of JR Cigar. Cede's expert argued that the tax rate was 36 percent, based on his review of the company's income statement. The company's expert utilized a 40 percent tax rate. The court accepted the company's expert's figure. In doing so, it noted that a footnote in the company's 1999 annual report explicitly stated that the tax rate ranged from 40.9 percent in 1997 to 40.2 percent in 1999. Thus, the court utilized a 40 percent tax rate.

After determining the contested factors, the court calculated the value of the company using the discounted cash flow method. It concluded that the fair value of the stock in JR Cigar was $13.58 per share on the valuation date.

Eateries, Inc. v. J.R. Simplot Co.

Tenth Circuit affirms experts' range of "typical" control premium

Case name: Citation: 2003 U.S. App. LEXIS 20349
Date of decision: October 6, 2003
Country: US
State or Federal: Federal
State/Jurisdiction: 10th Circuit
Court: United States Court of Appeals
Type of action: Tort
Experts: Mr. Payne
Mr. Wilsey
Mr. Davis
Judge: Brorby
SIC: 5812 Eating Places (full-service restaurants)

Key words: Damages, Breach of contract, Fair market value (FMV), Stock repurchase, Control premium

In this breach of contract action for salmonella contamination, the district court used a pre-contamination offer to purchase the company's assets as evidence of pre-contamination fair market value. It also accepted a later stock repurchase as evidence of post-contamination value, adding a control premium. The Tenth Circuit affirmed.

Facts

Eateries, Inc. was the sole shareholder of **Fiesta Restaurants, Inc.**, which owned and operated several **Garcia's Mexican Restaurants**. Eateries and Fiesta contracted with **J.R. Simplot Company** to provide Garcia's with chile rellenos. Some of the chile rellenos that Simplot delivered were contaminated with salmonella, and customers at four locations got sick. Extensive media coverage ensued.

A company called Halpern, Denny & Company had made a pre-contamination offer to buy Eateries' assets for $9.00 per share. However, the company withdrew its offer because of the contamination. It later made a new offer of $4.00 per share, which Eateries rejected.

About seven months after the contamination, Eateries repurchased the shares of a 27% shareholder for $5.125 per share. This repurchase price was the then-existing market price for the stock.

Eateries and Fiesta sued Simplot for breach of contract, and Simplot admitted liability, so the trial dealt solely with the issue of damages.

Valuation evidence

The court heard evidence from both parties' experts regarding a control premium for the Halpern Denny offer. One of Eateries' experts, **Mr. Payne,** calculated a 26.4% control premium for the Halpern Denny offer. One of Halpern Denny's general partners testified that the offer price represented a 6.7 market multiple, and the stock was trading about a 5.5 multiple. He also stated that the offer include some premium, although he did not calculate it.

Simplot's experts did not testify to a specific control premium for the Halpern Denny offer. Instead, **Mr. Wilsey** testified that a "normal" control premium was between 25 and 40%, and **Mr. Davis** testified that a "typical" control premium would be between 30 and 40%.

District court findings

The district court compared Eateries' fair market value before contamination with its fair market value after the contamination and awarded the difference as diminution in value damages to Eateries and Fiesta.

As evidence of pre-contamination value, the court used the $9.00 per-share offer by Halpern Denny. As evidence of the post-contamination value, the court accepted the $5.125 per-share repurchase price. It found, however, that the repurchase price did not include a control premium. Finding Mr. Davis's testimony most credible, and stating that "a premium of 30% to 40% is common," the court arrived at a value of $6.92 per share for the post-contamination value. It then subtracted $6.92 from $9.00 to find damages in the amount of $2.08 per share, or $8,200,697.40 for the 3,942,643 shares outstanding.

Holding on appeal and rationale

Both parties appealed. Simplot first argued that the district court erred in its valuation methodology and should have just calculated the difference between the public trading price of Eateries' stock before and after the contamination.

It claimed that the Halpern Denny offer was contingent and speculative. The Tenth Circuit Court of Appeals flatly rejected this argument, stating that Simplot's assertion contradicted the district court's findings and the testimony on record.

Simplot next argued that the stock repurchase did not reflect fair market value because it was a "forced purchase" and therefore did not involve a willing buyer and seller. The Tenth Circuit also dismissed this argument. Although it noted that the repurchase had been "privately negotiated," the court said that this did not indicate that the price was not "at least a good starting point for determining fair market value."

Eateries and Fiesta argued that the district court erred in adding a control premium because the repurchase price already included such premium. The court of appeals disagreed, referring to Eateries' president's testimony that the repurchase price was the current market price. "This indicates the repurchase price did not include a premium."

Alternatively, Eateries and Fiesta argued that the district court should have added no more than a 26.4% premium. They claimed that "it was error for the Court to rely on the most general estimates of potential control premiums when the Court had an actual control premium related to Eateries immediately before the damage." The Tenth Circuit was not swayed, however, and rejected their characterization of the expert's testimony as calculating an "actual" premium:

Their expert...did not and could not calculate a precise pre-contamination control premium because there was no set closing date for the sale to Halpern Denny. Instead, the experts estimated the control premium by averaging the high and low stock price during what he deemed the relevant time period.

The appellate court affirmed the district court on the diminution in value damages.

Framatome Connectors USA, Inc. and Subsidiaries, et al. v. CIR

Control Premium Considered

Date of decision: 1/16/2002

State or Federal: Federal

Type of action: Federal Taxation

In *Framatome Connectors USA, Inc. and Subsidiaries, et al. v. CIR*, 118 T.C. No. 3 (2002), the U.S. Tax Court considered whether Framatome's wholly owned subsidiary, Burndy-US, was entitled to claim its interest in Burndy-Japan as a controlled foreign corporation. Framatome USA, Inc. purchased Burndy-US in 1989 while it was expanding into the electrical connector business. In 1961, Burndy-US sought to enter the Japanese market. To that end, it formed Burndy-Japan with two Japanese companies. Each company received a 33.3 percent interest in Burndy-Japan. By 1973, Burndy-US sought to increase its interest in Burndy-Japan. Its partners each agreed to sell Burndy-US 8.3 percent of the company, raising Burndy-US's interest to 50 percent. The sale occurred at ′2,750 per share. However, as part of the sale, the shareholders entered into an agreement (the 1973 agreement) that included a restrictive transfer clause as well as enumerated a method for electing a board of directors favorable to the Japanese partners and required unanimous consent of the shareholders to declare dividends, sell or dissolve the company, or change the capital structure.

By the 1990s, Burndy-US was again disenchanted with its role in Burndy-Japan and sought to acquire a greater interest in the business. To that end, it engaged KPMG to value Burndy-Japan. Using 34 different methods, KPMG reported that Burndy-Japan had an average value of ′7,501 per share. The partners offered to sell their interest in Burndy-Japan for ′10,900 per share, but Burndy-US declined. The parties eventually negotiated a sale of 40 percent (20 percent from each partner) for ′8,750 per share. This raised Burndy-US's interest in Burndy Japan to 90 percent. As part of the sale, the parties renegotiated the 1973 agreement. This agreement (the 1993 agreement) gave Burndy-US operating control over Burndy-Japan. It removed many of the consensus provisions except for those involving a sale of the entire or an essential part of the business.

In 1987, Burndy-US began to treat Burndy-Japan as a controlled foreign corporation (CFC) for federal tax purposes.

In order to qualify as a CFC, a domestic corporation must control at least 50 percent of the voting power of the corporation; or hold at least 50 percent of the value of the corporation. The IRS audited the petitioners' tax return and disputed its treatment of Burndy-Japan as a CFC. The parties proceeded to the Tax Court for a determination of Burndy-Japan's tax treatment.

Before the Tax Court, both parties presented expert testimony regarding whether the company was a CFC. The court addressed the issue in two steps. It first considered whether Burndy-US controlled at least 50 percent of the voting power of Burndy-Japan. One aspect of the court's treatment of this question was whether Burndy-US had paid a control premium in its 1973 or 1993 acquisitions of Burndy-Japan stock.

The petitioners' expert concluded that a control premium had been paid in 1973, but had not been paid in 1993. He determined that a 12 percent control premium was paid in 1973 after considering the transaction price and 80 percent of the initial asking price. He used 80 percent after considering the 24 percent reduction in the Japanese shareholders' stake in the company. He additionally analyzed the 1973 transaction using an analogous company method. This expert then turned to the 1993 transaction. He looked at one of the 34 methods used by KPMG in estimating the value of the company in 1993. He selected an analogous company method, estimating the value of Burndy-Japan at '118 less per share than the 1993 selling price. This expert also considered the Japanese shareholders' offer to sell their interest in Burndy-Japan for '10,900 per share. The Tax Court rejected this expert's analysis. It found that his analogous company methods were not useful because the method was applied inconsistently with regard to the amount of data-this expert considered two years data with regard to the 1973 transaction and five years data with regard to the 1993 transaction. It concluded that he did not verify the accuracy of the data used in his treatment of the 1973 transaction. It lastly rejected his notion that the unconsummated offer to sell in 1993 was probative. It stated, "We infer nothing from ... [the] offer to sell because we do not know why ... [the Japanese shareholders] asked for payment of '10,900 per share, and because this unaccepted offer does not establish the fair market value of Burndy-Japan stock."

The IRS's first expert determined that a 30 percent control premium had been paid in connection with the 1993 transaction. In reaching this conclusion, the expert performed an independent valuation of the stock as well as considered the 1993 KPMG appraisal. The IRS's rebuttal expert also testified that many of the estimates contained in the 1993 KPMG appraisal fell below the 1993 transaction price. Based on this testimony and other evidence, the Tax Court concluded that Burndy-US did not pay a control premium in connection with its 1973 transaction but did with its 1993 transaction. The court concluded that in 1992 Burndy-US did not control at least 50 percent of Burndy-Japan.

The court then considered whether Burndy-US held at least 50 percent of the value of Burndy-Japan stock in 1992. Both parties presented expert testimony. The petitioners' expert argued that a control premium applied. The petitioners did not quantify the premium. They argued that any premium allotted to its 50 percent interest in Burndy-Japan gave Burndy-US more than 50 percent of the value of the company. The IRS's experts disagreed. They argued that discounts for lack of marketability and minority interest should apply. "They testified that a premium applies in valuing a large block of stock if the holder of that block has the power to extract private benefits that are disproportionate to benefits available to minority shareholders (private benefits analysis)." The petitioners argued that this method was not supported by published analyses or case law, but the Tax Court disagreed, noting several published sources discussing private benefits analyses. It then agreed with the IRS's experts that the petitioners were unable to extract private benefits from their 50 percent ownership interest. It stated, "Here, the veto provisions, supermajority requirements, and rules for electing directors increased the value of the Burndy-Japan stock held by ... [the Japanese shareholders] relative to the value of the stock held by Burndy-US and decreased the value of the Burndy-Japan stock held by Burndy-US relative to the value of the stock held by ... [the Japanese shareholders]." Thus, the court found that the Burndy-US's 50 percent interest in Burndy-Japan had a value of something less than 50 percent. Therefore, it concluded that Burndy-Japan did not qualify as a CFC in 1992.

Gagliano v. Brennan (I)

New Jersey follows Delaware law in dissenters' rights case

Citation: 344 N.J. Super. 83, 780 A.2d 553, 2001 N.J. Super. LEXIS 331
Date of decision: August 1, 2001
Country: US
State or Federal: State
State/Jurisdiction: New Jersey
Court: Court of Appeals
Type of action: Dissenting Shareholder
Experts: Donald Musso (for plaintiffs), David Budd (for plaintiffs), David Clarke (for plaintiffs), Robert Walters (for defendants), Christopher Hargrove (court-appointed)
Judge: Steinberg
SIC: 6712 Offices of Bank Holding Companies

Key words: Cash-out merger, Control premium, Fair dealing, Fair market value (FMV), Fair value, Fairness opinion

Plaintiff minority dissenting shareholders appealed, and defendant corporation cross-appealed, the trial court valuation of corporate stock.

Bank squeezes out minority

Amboy Bancorporation, a bank holding company, had one class of stock and one subsidiary, **Amboy National Bank** (collectively, Amboy). Amboy decided to reorganize to qualify for taxation as a Subchapter S corporation. It sent a proposed plan of the merger and a proxy to shareholders, providing for a cash-out of minority shareholders. After passage of the plan, certain shareholders sued, either individually or in class actions, alleging misrepresentation and failure to offer a fair price.

Experts give diverging valuations

Bank Advisory Group, Inc. (BAG) gave Amboy a financial fairness opinion in which it concluded that the price of $73 per share was "fair, from a financial standpoint, to all shareholders of the Company, including those shareholders receiving the Cash Consideration."

Robert Walters testified for defendants, stating that BAG used several different valuation approaches. BAG concluded that the fair cash value per share, for a minority interest of about 20% of Amboy's stock, was $69.50.

Certain individual plaintiffs obtained a fairness opinion and fair value report from **FinPro, Inc.** President and owner **Donald Musso** testified that he performed an acquisition valuation and agreed with BAG's acquisition-value result of $110 per share but disagreed with the 25% minority discount BAG used to reduce that result to $82.50 per share.

Another individual plaintiff retained **David Budd** of **McConnell Budd & Downs.** Budd criticized BAG's use of a minority discount and opined that the "appropriate value" of Amboy's stock was $120 per share. He testified to a number of different approaches, each indicating a value in excess of $73 per share.

The class action plaintiffs used **The Griffing Group** as their expert. Griffing's founder, **David Clarke**, testified that he also used different approaches. Under the guideline company approach, he valued the stock at $121.08 per share. He also considered the discounted cash flow method, under which he used Amboy's projections for asset growth and profitability to project Amboys "available or free cash flow" for 10 years and discounted it to a present value. Using that approach, he valued the stock at $117.40 per share. However, Clarke gave more weight to the guideline approach because it reflected "actual trading values" of the five guideline banks stock and ultimately concluded that Amboys adjusted fair market value was $120 per share.

The trial judge appointed an expert, **Christopher Hargrove**, to assist in determining fair value. He valued Amboy as a going concern, without marketability or minority discounts, and without a control premium. He also used a number of different approaches and derived a figure of $92.50 per share.

Trial court finds shareholders not offered fair value

The trial court concluded that the proxy contained misleading statements of material facts and failed to disclose all material facts about the true value and future prospects of Amboy and the true value of Amboys stock. Specifically, it found that the proxy was deficient for reciting the offered price without mentioning that it was derived by applying minority and marketability discounts, and also for failing to explain that the offered price was "fair market value" rather than "fair value."

The judge further determined that the representation that the price of $73 per share was fair to minority shareholders was misleading, erroneous, and incomplete, and that the vote of the consenting shareholders who approved the transaction was not a fully informed shareholder vote. The judge set a value of $90 per share.

Directors breached duty of fair dealing

The superior court, appellate division, stated that the record clearly supported the trial courts conclusion that the proxy statement was materially deficient and misleading regarding statements of value. Thus, it held that the directors breached their duty of fair dealing with the minority shareholders and therefore had the burden of proving that the price offered for the shares was fair.

Fair value does not include discounts

The trial court ruled that Amboy was to be valued as a going concern and that minority and marketability discounts and control premiums were prohibited as a matter of law. After reviewing New Jersey Supreme Court rulings, as well as looking to Delaware law for guidance, the superior court concluded that the trial court correctly declined to apply minority or marketability discounts to the shares.

Control premium permissible in appraisals

Delaware law does allow consideration of control premiums. However, the Delaware Supreme Court has cautioned that it may not be used as a vehicle to capture value of anticipated future effects of the merger. This would, in effect, allow an element of value representing expected synergies, which is prohibited by the Delaware statute.

Because New Jersey has a similar statute, the superior court concluded that in a valuation proceeding, a control premium should be considered in order to reflect market realities, provided it is not used to include the value of anticipated effects of the merger.

Because the trial court determined a control premium was prohibited as a matter of law, the superior court reversed and remanded with instructions to consider what, if any, control premium should be added to the value of the stock and what, if any, adjustments are necessary to exclude synergies.

Trial court erred in automatically rejecting valuations

The trial court rejected acquisition valuations because (1) they might include an element for anticipated synergies and (2) they would yield a corporations "sale value" rather than its value as a continuing business. Delaware law, however, permits any means of stock valuation as long as the technique is generally acceptable in the financial communities. Thus, courts may not exclude any valuation automatically. Of course, in the case of an acquisition valuation, there must be a correction for synergies.

The superior court also found that the trial court erred in automatically excluding from consideration several of the experts methods that contained an inherent control premium.

Consequently, the superior court reversed with instructions that the trial court must consider valuations that determine the acquisition value of Amboy as a going concern and that it may not automatically reject methods of valuation involving a control premium: "On remand, the parties shall be given the opportunity to explore and seek to develop a methodology to correct for the inherent minority discount, and exclude the element of synergies and future benefits before applying a control premium."

Gotham Partners, L.P. v. Hallwood Realty Partners, L.P., et al.

Sixteen Percent Control Premium Applied

Date of decision: 7/8/2003
Country: US
State or Federal: State
State/Jurisdiction: Delaware
Court: Court of Chancery
Type of action: Contract

In *Gotham Partners, L.P. v. Hallwood Realty Partners, L.P., et al.*, No. 15754 (Del. Ch. July 8, 2003), the Delaware Court of Chancery valued units in a real estate partnership that were acquired by the general partner's parent company in a transaction that breached the contractually-imposed entire fairness standard contained in the partnership agreement. In June 1995, the real estate partnership, which was publicly traded, acquired 293,539 of its units in a self-tender offer for $18.20 per unit. The acquired shares were then sold to the general partner's parent corporation at the same price. The sale to the parent corporation solidified the general partner's position because the parent corporation and its subsidiaries held enough units to block any attempt to remove the general partner. (Under the partnership agreement, a general partner could be removed by a two-thirds vote of the unit holders).

An earlier decision in this matter determined that Hallwood was liable for breaching the partnership agreement by failing to form an independent audit committee to review the transaction and to ensure that the terms of the transaction were "substantially equivalent to terms obtained by the partnership from a comparable third-party." The court determined that the transaction occurred at an unfair price considering the degree of control the corporate parent obtained in the transaction. However, the court found rescission to be inappropriate and considered a monetary award based on the value of the units. The Delaware Supreme Court determined that the Chancery Court's monetary award failed to properly account for a control premium. It then reversed and remanded for a redetermination of the monetary award.

Gotham did not present any testimony as to the value of the real estate partnership on the date of the transaction. Hallwood presented an expert who valued the partnership using the comparable company, discounted cashflow and net asset value methods. The court primarily relied upon the testimony of Hallwood's expert in determining the value of the partnership.

In performing his comparable company transaction, Hallwood's expert selected comparables based on four criteria: (1) the business was a domestic business owning and operating income producing properties; (2) the business was publicly traded at a price of $2 per unit or greater; (3) the business had annual revenues of at least $25 million; and (4) the business did not make cash distributions of 3 percent or greater. Gotham challenged the inclusion of businesses meeting the fourth criteria. Gotham argued that the fourth factor was irrelevant. The Delaware Chancery Court disagreed. It found that companies making smaller distributions traded at larger discounts to net asset value. It further noted that the partnership at issue had not made any distributions and was not in a position to do so in the near future on the valuation date. Therefore, the Chancery Court agreed with Hallwood's expert's criteria for selecting comparable companies. However, it did disagree with the expert with regard to two companies that were excluded from the expert's universe of comparables. After considering those companies, the Chancery Court determined that the comparables indicated a median multiple of 10 to the last twelve months EBITDA. This was reduced to 9.5 times the previous twelve months EBITDA to account for the subject company's relative weakness in comparison to the comparables. Under this method, the court determined that each unit had a value of $36.16.

In making his discounted cash flow method valuation, Hallwood's expert rejected the subject company's beta of 0.63 because "the thin trading in Partnership units and other market factors made the Partnership's beta an unreliable factor in determining the cost of capital." Therefore, the expert calculated a beta based on comparable companies, which he calculated into a leveraged beta to account for the partnership's capital structure. He concluded that a beta of 3.35 was appropriate. He next applied a 3 percent company specific risk premium and a 4 percent small stock risk premium adjustment to his calculation of the cost of equity. He concluded that a 38 percent cost of equity was appropriate. He also determined that the cost of debt was 9 percent. He therefore concluded that the weighted cost of capital (WACC) was 13 percent. Gotham challenged the calculation of the cost of equity. The Chancery Court stated, "Given what Gotham itself contends was an 'inefficient' market in the Partnership's units and given the heavy debt the Partnership carried, the judgment that the Partnership's published beta was out of line strikes me as reasonable." However, the court rejected the application of the risk premiums. It found, "The adjustment to beta alone was sufficient to account adequately for those factors." Removing the risk premiums reduced the WACC to 12 percent and resulted in a per unit price of $35.

Both parties presented some evidence of the appropriate net asset value calculation. Gotham argued, through its real estate investment trust (REIT) expert, that no discount from net asset value was appropriate based on evidence from REITs.

Hallwood's expert determined that a 60 percent discount from net asset value was appropriate. His discount was based on comparable companies. The court rejected both experts. It found that the REIT data did not support a zero discount from net asset value because REITs were not comparable to the subject real estate partnership. Moreover, it found that if the requirements used to determine a zero discount for REITs was applied to the subject partnership, that criteria indicated that a large discount from net asset value would be warranted. However, it found Hallwood's expert's 60 percent discount too large. It stated, "[T]his discount is too great given the Partnership's listing on a major exchange and its improving performance." Thus, the court relied upon a report provided by Gotham in an earlier trial. This report indicated that a discount from net asset value of 36 percent was appropriate. The discount was determined based on a review of tender offers. Using the 36 percent discount, the court concluded that, under this method, the per unit price was $38.86.

The court lastly considered the market price of the units. It stated, "Whether or not the Partnership's units were thinly traded, they were listed on a major exchange. ... In the real world, market prices matter and are usually considered the best evidence of value. And they should matter in formulating a remedy in this case." In making this ruling, the court particularly noted that the general partner could have made a non-coercive tender offer with full disclosure and not been forced to pay a high premium in the market.

The Chancery Court then averaged the results of the aforementioned methods. It determined that the partnership units had a minority, marketable value of $31.06 per unit. It then considered the application of a control premium. It accepted the analysis of Hallwood's expert. This expert reviewed transactions involving a change in control of real estate partnerships during the pertinent period. This review indicated a median premium of 16 percent over the market price. The court then applied this premium to the per unit price, to determine that each unit acquired in the contested transaction had a value of $36.02. The court noted that this price was 154 percent of the unit's market value. It further noted, "Gotham has failed to present evidence that transactions at this level occur in the real world." It then deducted the purchase price of the units from the value of the units as determined by the court, and ordered damages of $21.82 per share plus interest.

Highfields Capital, Ltd. v. AXA Financial, Inc.

Del. Chancery Rejects DCF Analysis in Insurance Co. Appraisal

Citation: 2007 Del. Ch. LEXIS 126
Date of decision: August 17, 2007
Country: US
State or Federal: State
State/Jurisdiction: Delaware
Court: Court of Chancery
Type of action: Dissenting Shareholder
Experts: Dr. Israel Shaked (petitioner); Peter C. Jachym (respondent)
Judge: Lamb
SIC: 6311 -- Specific categories --

This is yet another judicial appraisal action where the Delaware Chancery Court is less than satisfied with the widely disparate valuations offered by the litigants, and exercises its "independent business judgment" in crafting the final calculations, albeit relying on the more credible of the two expert reports. The Court also departs from its typical preference for the discounted cash flow (DCF) method where the merger price rose from an arm's-length transaction and industry standards favor a different analysis.

MONY ripe for merger

To remain competitive amidst the consolidation of the insurance industry in the 1990s, the Mutual of New York life insurance company "demutualized," and in 1998, its successor, the MONY Group, Inc. (MONY) completed a public offering at $23.50 per share. Despite substantial efforts to diversify, MONY's earnings and return on equity lagged significantly behind those of its peers. Considerable pressure from insurance ratings agencies further depressed its earnings, capital, and liquidity, eventually leading to a ratings downgrade in late 2002. MONY management instituted a long-range cost-cutting and restructuring plan and obtained a third-party actuarial appraisal to assist these efforts and help attract a merger partner or sale.

By this time, the industry and investment communities "all understood that MONY's days as a stand-alone were numbered," especially since New York insurance regulations requiring state approval for acquisitions in the company greater than 5% were due to expire. For the year 2002 to

2003, only one potential buyer, AXA Financial, Inc. (AXA) approached MONY. After lengthy negotiations, it offered $31.00 per share, a 7.3% premium over MONY's then-trading price. Several institutional investors criticized the price as too low, but others compared MONY's 2% return on equity to the industry average of 12% and found the price fair. Management feared the company faced a "meltdown" absent the transaction, and after consulting its legal and financial advisors, the Board approved and announced the merger in September 2003.

One of the institutional investors, Highfields Capital, Ltd. and its affiliates (Highfields)—which held 4.3% of MONY common stock—tried to enjoin the merger. It submitted a letter urging the Del. Chancery to abridge the vote of MONY stockholders who held "long" positions in the securities underwriting the transaction. What Highfields neglected to reveal was its own substantial "short" position on the securities, on which it stood to make $11 million should the merger fail.

The Court declined to grant the injunction, finding that MONY Board's acted in good faith. But the growing uncertainty caused MONY to suffer another ratings downgrade in February 2004. No other buyer came forward, and the stockholders finally approved the merger by 51%. After it closed in July 2004, Highfields was the only major stockholder to perfect its appraisal rights in the Delaware Chancery Court.

Highfields disputes merger price

The familiar "fair value" premise in judicial appraisal actions comprises a company's standalone value, excluding any shared synergies with a potential acquirer. If the subject transaction resulted from arm's-length bargaining between independent parties, "and if no structural impediments existed that might materially distort the crucible of objective market reality," the Court explained, then the merger price carries substantial weight as an indicator of fair value.

Under this standard, Highfields asserted that the $31 merger price was an unreliable indicator of MONY's fair value. It offered a financial expert who opined that factors such as management's financial incentives and its failure to open the auction to all bidders in the beginning "distorted the sale process in AXA's favor." But its case-in-chief consisted of valuation testimony from a finance professor who applied four different approaches to appraising MONY and the merger price:

1. *DCF.* In his DCF analysis, the expert relied on August 2003 management projections, believing these to better indicate standalone value than February 2004 projections, which followed the ratings downgrade. He used GAAP earnings to generate free cash flows; a 5% terminal growth rate, derived from an institutional investor database; and a 8.9% discount rate from CAPM to reach a $39.18 per-share value. He gave a 50% weight to this DCF value in his overall analysis.

2. *Comparable company analysis.* Thirteen comparable companies emerged from the expert's review of the S&P Life and Health Insurance (L&H) Index and also a list identified by MONY's investment advisor. Using a price-to-book multiple, which was more typical for the insurance industry than a price-to-earnings multiple, he derived a 0.89 multiple for MONY from the lower quartile of guideline companies. After applying a 30.1% minority discount, derived from transactions data, he arrived at a $46.69 value, weighted 30% overall.

3. *Comparable transactions analysis.* The expert found seven transactions in the life insurance industry from 1999 to 2004 where at least 51% of the target was acquired for more than $200 million. Based on price-to-book value, he assigned MONY a 1.37 multiple in the lower quartile of the data. After removing a 14.5% synergy premium from the MONY merger, he arrived at a $47.15 per-share value, weighted 20% overall.

4. *Market price analysis.* The Highfields' expert examined how the market would have priced MONY stock had the merger price not effectively acted as a cap. He took MONY's stock price a month prior to the merger ($28.20), adjusted for a minority discount, and multiplied by MONY's expected 15.1% return rate (derived from the L&H index's 21.7% appreciation during the same time and using a beta of 0.69). This resulted in a $42.22, control-basis, "expected unaffected price" as of the merger date. The expert also conducted an event study/volume analysis on MONY stock at the time of the merger announcement and found no statistically relevant fluctuations in price or volume.

Shared synergies and actuarial analysis

AXA enlisted expert testimony from the managing director of a boutique investment bank that focused exclusively on the financial services industry. He used five metrics to value MONY:

1. *Shared synergies.* The merger price ($31.00 per share) minus the synergies that AXA would develop from the transaction ($7.75 per share) was the best indicator of the company's going concern value, or $23.75 per share. No material impediments existed to a competing bid, the expert said, and materials from the Board's valuation process supported the analysis, including the February 2004 (post-downgrade) projections. The company was already at the bottom or the industry, and any further downgrade would significantly depress the only area in which MONY was still achieving sales. The expert ascribed an overall weight of 50% to this analysis.

2. *Sum of the parts.* Because MONY consisted of three segments (insurance, brokerage, and asset management), the next best method was an actuarial, sum-of-the-parts analysis. The insurance business also consisted of three components: i) net asset value, which the expert derived from MONY's statutory (as opposed to GAAP) earnings; and ii) in-force and iii) future business values, derived from projections that AXA used to develop its bid. For the brokerage business, the expert used a comparable companies analysis but not a DCF, due to lack of reliable projections; he did use a weighted average of both approaches to value the asset management business. Overall, he concluded a $17.68 per share value using the actuarial approach, weighted 35%.

3. *Comparable companies.* The expert selected publicly traded life insurance companies with market capitalization between $500 million and $5 billion, and then analyzed each firm's price-to-book, and price-to-estimated-earnings for both 2004 and 2005. Statistically, MONY was the "worst-performing and most troubled company" of its peer group, he found. After eliminating a 16.1% implied minority discount, he arrived at a $19.98 per-share value, weighting it only 7.5%.

4. *Comparable transactions.* After selecting six acquisitions of insurance companies between 2001 and mid-2004, the expert assigned a 10% weight to all but one—a sale of Safeco, a life insurance company that struggled with low returns, was operationally similar to MONY, and was sold three months before the AXA-MONY merger. Safeco's sale price was slightly less than MONY's, but after applying a 16.1% "synergies" discount, the expert weighted the transaction 50%. In his overall transactions analysis, he ultimately derived a $18.83 per-share value, giving it a 5% weight.

5. *DCF.* AXA's expert characterized his 10% discount rate as "aggressive," benchmarked against discount rates used in proxy statements for financial transactions between 1999 and 2004. He also criticized the use of GAAP earnings in Highfields' expert's DCF analysis, and used data that MONY prepared to meet statutory accounting requirements. His DCF value was $21.38 per-share, with a 2.5% weight overall.

Experts 'two ships passing in the night'

The parties' divergent valuations struck the Court as "two ships passing in the night," with each party showing equal "tedium in attacking (often with good cause) every assumption used or conclusion reached by the other party's expert." Generally, the Court found the metrics used by AXA's expert—in particular the shared synergies and actuarial analyses—to be more credible.

Strikingly, despite the industry standard of using a sum-of-the-parts...appraisal methodology to value an insurance conglomerate as a going concern, and despite the reliance this court typically places on the merger price in an appraisal proceeding that arises from an arm's length transaction, [Highfields' expert] provided no testimony about MONY's value pursuant to these important models. [His] valuation not only suffers because of these analytical gaps, it is also markedly disparate from market price data for MONY's stock and other independent indicia of value.

For the same reasons, the Court also discredited the reliance Highfields' expert placed on his DCF analysis. For an insurance company, subject to statutory limits on distributions, GAAP earnings were not the appropriate basis by which to project free cash flows. The expert also used a constant growth rate beginning in 2005 without presenting any evidence that the company would be able to stabilize its future earnings. By relying on the August 2003 (pre-downgrade) projections, he "completely ignore[d] the fundamental nature" of MONY's situation. "Indeed, [his] DCF becomes nothing more than an extension of 2005 financial projections in which MONY's calculated terminal value represents almost 100% of [the expert's] total estimated value of the company."

By contrast, AXA's expert did not rely on outdated projections, and he used estimated statutory earnings as a cash flow proxy. More he importantly, as an analyst in the financial services sector, more importantly recognized that the insurance industry does not consider a DCF an important or useful framework, assigning it a mere 2.5% weight in his overall analysis. The Court agreed, noting that in this case, it would not use a pure DCF methodology in determining MONY's value.

Guideline public company methods suffer

Likewise, the Court did not give much weight to the guideline public companies analysis in this case. The companies selected by Highfields' expert were not sufficiently comparable to MONY. Further, the expert placed MONY at the median of the bottom quartile and assigned it a multiple of 0.89x using a price-to-book value metric. This represented a 27% discount from his comparable company medium and a 33% discount from the mean, more evidence that his analysis was "overly biased and subjective." Finally, his calculation of a 30.1% control premium was "questionable" because he relied on a pool of dissimilar transactions and ignored the synergies that financial buyers could enjoy from their acquisitions.

By contrast, AXA's expert conceded the lack of comparability between MONY and publicly traded life insurance companies, assigning this method a minor (7.5%) weight. But his analysis suffered similar flaws; i.e., using a price-to-book multiple that was a substantial discount (40%) from both the median and the mean. He also relied heavily on price-to-estimated earnings multiples when he testified that neither the market nor the insurance industry would typically value MONY on an earnings basis.

In light of the shortcomings of both experts, the Court rejected the comparable companies analysis, as it did the comparable transactions. The Highfields' expert used aged transactions, the majority five years removed from the AXA-MONY merger. He relied on non-comparable transactions while excluding the one real comparable—the Safeco sale. In post-trial briefing, Highfields tried belatedly to include Safeco in the expert's transaction analysis, but the Court found the effort "procedurally inappropriate," casting "great doubt" on the expert's objectivity.

AXA's expert didn't fare much better. In his transactions analysis, he relied on an implied price-to-earnings multiple of 12.5x, which resulted in a $4.50 per share value. The Court found "no conceivable basis" to assign any weight to such an "outlying value of MONY," yet the expert weighted it 30%. Further, he failed to adjust the price-to-book metric for each selected company's unrealized capital gains and losses, per SFAS 115.

The expert assigned a 0.53x price-to-book value multiple for the Safeco transaction, for example, but conceded that with SFAS 115 adjustments, the multiple would be 0.73x. The adjusted values were not publicly available for half of his selected transactions, and the expert's analysis could not recover from this "irreparable structural malady."

Market and merger price analyses

"Overwhelming evidence" showed that the market was well aware of MONY's merger prospects for a long time, including the date of the announcement (September 2003), when most likely the market price already reflected a merger speculation premium. Thus, the event and volume studies by Highfields' expert were not particularly meaningful when such an imbedded condition exists.

Moreover, his assumption that MONY's stock price would move in direct proportion to the L&H index was highly speculative, as MONY historically underperformed the index, and three of the seven companies on the list weren't comparable. AXA's expert criticized the indexing as "unprecedented" in the financial community, and the Court agreed, citing cases in which it had "considered, and rejected, the explanatory power of a similar model." Finally, the Highfields' expert incorrectly assumed that the merger price acted as a ceiling on MONY's stock value, when in reality, it served as a floor. "If the going-concern value of MONY was somehow depressed by AXA's bid during a time of highly favorite market conditions, the emergence of a topping bid would be all the more probable," including one by Highfields.

Further, the AXA-MONY merger negotiations were "clearly" arm's-length; no MONY officer or director participated in the buy-side, and none continued employment at the company after the merger closed. The three directors who would receive any change-in-control payments recused themselves from the merger vote. Given these facts, the reason why the merger proceeded was self-evident: No other strategic or financial buyer stood to gain the synergies that AXA anticipated in acquiring MONY at $31 per share.

To determine the amount of shared synergies imbedded in the price, the Court first looked to the evidence offered by AXA's expert. But contrary to his own testimony, he largely relied on a DCF analysis to conclude that shared synergies constituted 25%—or $7.75—of the merger price. The Court found the assumptions in his "sum of the parts" analysis more credible, which drew from the independent actuarial valuation performed at the merger announcement and viewed shared synergies at $9.54 per share. But AXA's actuarial analysis at the merger closing revealed a loss of $5.42 per share in synergies. The Court deducted the difference of $4.12 and found that $26.88 was the fair value merger price, according this analysis a 75% weight.

AXA's "sum of the parts" analysis also proved reliable, especially with respect to MONY's life insurance and asset-management businesses. Its expert erred by not placing forward-looking earnings metrics in his valuation of the broker-dealer business, and the Court removed these outliers. Overall, it concluded a $19.22 per-share value under the actuarial analysis, to which it assigned a 25% weight.

Given this comprehensive overview, the Court's conclusions and their respective weightings, it appraised the fair value of MONY at the time of the merger at $24.97 per share.

Lane v. Cancer Treatment Centers of America, Inc.

Delaware critiques conventional BV models for valuing an emerging, short-lived niche company, but goes with DCF

Citation: 2004 Del. Ch. LEXIS 108
Date of decision: July 30, 2004
Country: US
State or Federal: State
State/Jurisdiction: Delaware
Court: Court of Chancery
Type of action: Dissenting Shareholder
Experts: Robert Robert J. Cimasi (for dissenting shareholder), Richard S. Baehr (for corporation)
Judge: Noble
SIC: 8069 Specialty Hospitals, Except Psychiatric (except children's and substance abuse hospitals)

The issue in this appraisal action, filed by **Robert Michael Lane**, was the fair value of the common stock of **Cancer Treatment Centers of America, Inc.** ("CTCA" or the "Company"), as of March 20, 1991 (the "Merger Date"), the date on which CTCA merged (the "Merger") into **RSJ, Inc.** (RSJ). Lane owned 100 shares of CTCA common stock, which represented 10% of CTCA's outstanding shares of common. Under the merger agreement, Lane was to receive $260.00 per share, but he objected that this merger consideration was inadequate.

Valuation summary

As the court noted, "All too often in appraisal actions, the Court is presented with two competing experts espousing 'wildly divergent' interpretations of the circumstances confronting the corporation." This case was no exception. Lane's expert, **Robert J. Cimasi**, contended that the fair value of CTCA was $16,400,000 as of the merger date. In stark contrast, CTCA's expert, **Richard S. Baehr**, concluded that the fair value of CTCA was zero.

Cimasi utilized three approaches to determine the fair value of CTCA: discounted cash flow (DCF) analysis, a comparable transactions method, and a guideline publicly traded company method. Cimasi then assigned the resulting fair values generated by each method a weight he deemed appropriate and calculated a weighted average to arrive at the fair value for the common stock of CTCA. Baehr used only DCF. The court expressed reservations about using any of these methods, and declined to accept either expert's estimation of value, but nevertheless made an independent valuation using DCF and concluded that CTCA was worth $1,345,000 on the valuation date.

Background

Lane was hired to—and did—revitalize **American International Hospital** (AIH), which is controlled by **Richard Stephenson.** Lane, an experienced hospital administrator, along with Stephenson, **Randall L. Pittman** and **Robert Mayo** (Mayo) agreed to create CTCA as a Subchapter S corporation. The plan was to reverse the decline of AIH and then use the funds generated by a resurgent AIH to build a national cancer care network of between 12 and 20 treatment centers.

The CTCA business model sought to capture a niche in the cancer treatment market, namely, those pre-treated cancer patients who had failed their initial round(s) of cancer treatment. CTCA sought not only to supply outsourcing services to, but also to own and operate the facilities of, a national network of cancer treatment centers. Under a Management Services Agreement (the "MSA"), CTCA was compensated for services provided to AIH on the basis of actual costs plus a 20% markup.

CTCA also founded **Memorial Medical Center** and **Cancer Institute, Inc.** (MMC), a treatment center initially funded by MSA payments from AIH. MMC turned out to be a disastrous business venture that suffered from grave losses and had a net capital deficiency that raised substantial doubt about its ability to continue as a going concern. CTCA foundered, and, eventually, merged into RSJ, an entity wholly owned by Stephenson. In a separate appraisal action relating to MMC's merger into an RSJ subsidiary, an Oklahoma court ruled that MMC had no value.

Cimasi's general assumptions

Although Cimasi recognized the existence of certain negative macroeconomic and industry trends, Cimasi concluded optimistically that any impact upon CTCA would be negligible and that the average daily census (ADC) for cancer patients at its facilities would increase. Cimasi predicted growth at the Company's treatment centers, and also predicted that CTCA would establish three new cancer treatment centers within the next five years, a projection he characterized as "conservative." He also concluded that the MSA, with its 20% return over costs, would remain in place for the foreseeable future.

Cimasi's DCF

Working from these general assumptions, Cimasi predicted the performance of CTCA over a five-year interval be ginning immediately after the Merger Date. He calculated revenues by marking up expenses by 20% and allocating the resulting revenue figure to the individual centers.

To derive projected expenses, Cimasi presented various growth rates regarding different categories of expenses extrapolated from historical data. After arriving at net income, he calculated projected yearly cash flows. Cimasi then added net income amounts for the non-cash expenses of depreciation and amortization. Next, Cimasi adjusted the resulting figure for increases in working capital and fixed assets.

Thus, Cimasi arrived at a projected net cash flow for each of the five projected years following the merger date. These projected values substantially deviated from those projected by Baehr due to the assumption of the opening of the operated centers. Cimasi then discounted his projections by a Weighted Average Cost of Capital (WACC) equal to 27.43%. Cimasi determined a discount rate through the Adjusted Capital Asset Pricing Model (ACAPM). For a terminal value, Cimasi increased (by 5%) the net cash flow of projected year 5, and assumed that this amount, with an annual growth rate of 5%, would be returned in perpetuity.

Cimasi next capitalized the projected terminal cash flow by 22.43%. This terminal value was then discounted accordingly (at 27.43%) to arrive at a fully discounted (as of the merger date) terminal value. With the summation of these discounted cash flows, Cimasi derived a present fair value of the business enterprise of $18,309,901.

Cimasi includes control premium

Cimasi next departed significantly from the analysis of Baehr and included a "control premium." The control premium, Cimasi claimed, was justified because of the inclusion of an inherent minority discount due to the use of market prices in establishing the WACC. Accordingly, Cimasi added 20% of the present fair value of the business enterprise ($3,661,980) to the present fair value of the business enterprise to arrive at a total present fair value of the business enterprise of $21,971,881. To determine the present fair value of CTCA, Cimasi subtracted $4,052,300 in interest bearing debt and arrived at $17,920 per share.

Comparable transaction method

In addition to relying upon the DCF analysis, Cimasi also employed the comparable transaction method. Using this method, using as comparables selected hospital management and specialty hospital companies, Cimasi computed a fair value for CTCA of $9,836,000, or $9,836 per share.

Guideline publicly traded companies method

The final method utilized by Cimasi was the guideline publicly traded companies method. Pursuant to this approach, Cimasi selected comparable companies that were categorized in the same Standard Industrial Classification (SIC) Code as CTCA. For the set of comparable companies, Cimasi then calculated the weighted price-to-revenue, weighted price-to-EBITDA, weighted total invested capital (TIC), and weighted TIC-to-EBITDA ratios; he then chose to rely equally upon only the weighted TIC and weighted TIC-to-EBITDA ratios.

Analyzing both the data presented in the 10K and 10Q reports of the chosen comparable companies, and again applying a 20% adjustment to correct for a perceived minority discount inherent in market-based price data, Cimasi averaged the two values so derived. The result was a fair value for CTCA of $18,259,000, or $18,259 per share.

Cimasi's fair value estimation

Cimasi afforded the DCF analysis a 50% weighting, the comparable transactions approach a 20% weighting and the comparable companies approach a 30% weighting. The end result was a fair value for CTCA as of the Merger Date of $16,400,000, or $16,400 per share.

Baehr's analysis

Baehr, like Cimasi, explored macroeconomic and industry trends, noting that as of the merger date the economy was in a recession. Citing, among other things, an established trend toward outpatient care, and overall increased competition between cancer treatment institutions for both regional and local market share, his assumptions were that MMC was in a downward spiral, and that CTCA would open no new facilities. He also predicted that MSA payments from AIH, which he observed faced great uncertainty, would not continue indefinitely at a 20% rate.

Baehr uses only DCF

Unlike Cimasi, Baehr used only a DCF analysis to determine a fair value for CTCA. He posited four different possible scenarios for CTCA and calculated DCF for each scenario. He projected operating expenses, then deducted interest and depreciation, then deducted taxes at a tax rate of 38%. To derive cash flow, Baehr added back depreciation and amortization and also added back interest expense. Baehr finally adjusted the amount thus derived to provide for capital expenditures in each projected year and changes in working capital. Having done so, Baehr arrived at a projected net cash flow. Baehr proceeded to discount the projected stream of net cash flows.

Baehr calculated a WACC of 27.9% using the Capital Asset Pricing Model (CAPM). In all but one of the scenarios, Baehr derived a negative value for CTCA. Given that he concluded that the assumptions underlying the other scenario were implausible, he concluded that that CTCA had a going concern value of $0 as of the merger date.

Court's holding and rationale

The court, indicating that both experts' analyses were flawed, independently calculated the fair value of CTCA under a DCF approach and assessed the usefulness of the comparable companies and transactions approaches.

As to areas that the parties significantly disagreed on, the court concluded that the MSA was in reality a financing vehicle that would continue indefinitely, but that after 3 years, the rate would go down to 15%. The court also agreed with Lane that, based upon the evidence as of the merger date, MMC would continue to operate for the foreseeable future. Additionally, the court determined that MMC, while having no value, could best be modeled as paying current obligations, but never earning a profit. Accordingly, the court concluded that MMC would not be able to repay debt it owed to CTCA and that compensation afforded to CTCA for its services would remain at cost—not, as Cimasi assumed, increase to levels under the MSA. Finally, the court determined that CTCA would be financially unable to expand in the foreseeable future.

Saying that "[o]ne can reasonably have doubts about the ability of a DCF analysis to capture accurately the fair value of an emerging company with an earnings history of less than two years," the court essentially adopted Baehr's model, because it found it to be the more reasonable of the two presented. The court, however, deviated from his approach in the projection of costs, the estimate of long-term growth, and the terms of the MSA to incorporate its determinations as to the business reality facing CTCA at the time of the merger.

This DCF model showed that CTCA had a value of $1,008,000 as a going concern as of the merger date. Because there was only a modest difference between the two calculations of WACC between Cimasi and Baehr, the court accepted as reasonable the capital structure used by both experts, and, finding that Baehr's methodology and inputs for determining the cost of equity were better factually supported, the court utilized Baehr's calculated WACC of 27.9%. Applying this discount rate, the court calculated that the present value of the terminal value of CTCA was $1,334,000.

Citing Pratt, *Business Valuation Discounts And Premiums*, the court rejected Cimasi's addition of a 20% control premium, asserting that the belief that the income approach always produces a publicly traded minority basis of value "is a very common and highly flawed conclusion."

The court also observed that many distinguishing features (e.g., niche company in a narrow field) of CTCA impaired comparison to publicly traded companies and thereby frustrated any attempt to measure value by using the comparable companies analyses. Finally, applying a weighting of 85% for the DCF analysis and 15% for the comparable companies analysis, the court held that fair value of CTCA, as of the merger date, was $1,345,000 or $1,345 a share.

Court's concluding thoughts

The court made a point of adding the following dicta: "[an] aspect of this case which is worthy of comment is the uncertain capacity of the typically employed financial models to capture the value of an emerging, niche market company." The court emphasized that CTCA's unique situation—contracts with affiliated entities, very short track record, being a unique concept in a unique market—may have significantly restricted the usefulness of the tools commonly used to determine fair value."

Estate of Mary D. Maggos v. CIR

Earnings Methods Used to Value Pepsi-Cola Bottler

Date of decision: 4/11/2000

State or Federal: Federal

Type of action: Estate and Gift Taxation

In *the* T.C. Memo. 2000-129, the Tax Court considered the value of a Pepsi-Cola bottling company for the purposes of the gift tax. During her life the decedent and her son operated Pepsi-Cola Alton Bottling, Inc. (PCAB). The decedent held a 56.7 percent (567 shares) interest in the corporation. This interest provided the decedent with operating control of the corporation. Her son held the remaining shares in the corporation and operated the company. As part of her estate plan, the decedent and her son entered into a transaction in May 1987 where the company redeemed her interest in exchange for a $3 million promissory note. As a result of this transaction, the decedent's son became the sole shareholder in PCAB. No gift tax return was filed pursuant to this transaction, no valuation of the stock was performed prior to this transaction, and the parties did not negotiate regarding the price. Two years later, the son sold the business for $12.9 million. When the decedent died in 1996, she bequeathed the promissory note to her son.

Upon a review of the estate tax return, the Service valued the stock redeemed in the 1987 transaction and found that the fair market value of the decedent's interest was $8,056,000. It determined that the decedent made a gift to her son in the 1987 transaction, and sought the additional tax. The estate countered that the decedent lacked the donative intent necessary to make a gift or that the transaction was a bad business decision. It alternatively argued that the fair market value of the stock was not in excess of the value of the promissory note. The parties made these arguments before the Tax Court, where they presented valuation evidence.

The Tax Court began by finding that the decedent did make a gift to her son in the transaction. The court found that the "decedent was not concerned with and did not negotiate or authorize her attorney to negotiate for the fair market value of her interest in PCAB. The price received was the price that satisfied decedent's needs while she was alive, was the greatest amount her son believed he could pay, and was the lowest price... [Her son's] lawyers thought could be defended for gift tax purposes. So long as the transaction could be defended for Federal gift tax purposes, the fair market value of the PCAB shares that were redeemed was not of material concern to decedent." The court then noted that for the purposes of the gift tax, the value of the gift is determined by subtracting the amount received from the fair market value of the asset on the date of transfer. It then turned to the valuation evidence.

The IRS' expert was an accredited senior member of the American Society of Appraisers. He valued the decedent's interest using four valuation methods and concluded that the fair market value of the stock was $7,938,000. The IRS' expert used the 1989 sale of PCAB as a reality check for his value. The court found significant errors in this expert's valuation. The court rejected his public guideline company and the market transaction method valuations. It found that the comparable companies used under both approaches were not comparable in size or in operations. All the companies were quite large and did not have the high percentage of resale of products bottled elsewhere which PCAB had. The Tax Court next valued the decedent's interest in PCAB using the discounted cash flow method. As part of this method, the decedent's expert used the weighted average cost of capital (WACC) and the capital asset pricing model (CAPM). This expert determined that the appropriate beta was 0.76, which provided a cost of equity of 14.2 percent. He then determined the pre-tax cost of debt to be 10.5 percent. He also determined that the residual value of PCAB 10 years in the future would be 12.5 times its net earnings. Furthermore, this expert made certain adjustments to PCAB's cash flow. He added back an amount for the amortization of intangibles. He concluded that the sale of the decedent's interest would be a qualified stock purchase under IRC sec. 338 which would allow the purchaser to amortize the franchise agreement under IRC sec. 1253. He also added back the corporation's working capital in excess of $100,000 ($366,744) and deferred charges ($243,031). (This expert also made an adjustment for shareholder loans the company made to the decedent's son, however his treatment of those loans is unclear from the case).

The taxpayer also presented expert valuation testimony. It's expert used only the capitalization of cash flow method to determine its value, $2,691,458. This expert concluded that a market approach was inapplicable because there were no similar companies and because PCAB was "a small, atypical Pepsi bottler." This expert further rejected the discounted cash flow method "because of difficulties in forecasting future revenues and earnings, given significant changes in margins and earnings in the years preceding the Valuation Date." This expert made similar adjustments, as the IRS' expert did, to PCAB's cash flow. Lastly, this expert applied a 25 percent discount for lack of marketability. The IRS criticized this expert's valuation because he failed to reduce the amount of compensation ($250,000) the son received from the corporation. It argued that the son's compensation would be adjusted to $100,000 per year if the decedent's interest were sold to an unrelated purchaser. The Tax Court agreed with this criticism.

The taxpayer also presented an additional expert who testified to the appropriate discount for lack of marketability and the applicable control premium. This expert concluded a 30 percent liquidity discount should be applied. He additionally determined that the average control premium paid in the beverage industry during the 10 years preceding the transaction was 35.84 percent. He argued however "that the minority shareholder would have to consent to any sale, and therefore the control premium should be turned into a discount because the majority shareholder would need to pay the minority shareholder to get that consent."

The Tax Court considered both experts' valuations. It found various errors with both experts. As noted earlier, the court rejected the IRS' valuations using the public guideline company and the comparable transactions methods. The court also rejected this expert's use of the discounted cash flow method, and his calculation of WACC and CAPM. The court cited *Furman v. Commissioner*, T.C. Memo. 1998-157, which holds that CAPM and WACC are not the proper analytical tools for valuing small closely held corporations with little chance of going public. It then found errors with the expert's use of CAPM. It stated, "We are not persuaded that the guideline companies used ... to determine beta in this case were appropriate. None of the companies selected were shown to have had operations that were substantially similar to PCAB. Nor are we persuaded that PCAB should be assigned a smaller beta than the guideline companies assuming that they were appropriate." The court next took issue with this expert's cost of debt. The court could find no rationale why a hypothetical purchaser "could obtain a debt rate less than 2 percent above the Government bond rate." The court also received evidence from the IRS that this expert failed to include a small company risk premium. The Service noted that had the risk premium been included, the capitalization rate would have been at least 17.5 percent. The court additionally rejected this expert's adjustments to PCAB's cash flow. The court also rejected similar adjustments in the taxpayer's capitalization of cash flow method. After adjustments to both the taxpayer's capitalization of cash flows and the IRS' discounted cash flow methods, the court recalculated the discounted cash flow method and determined that the fair market value of the decedent's 56.7 percent interest was approximately $4.9 million on a marketable minority basis. It then considered appropriate discounts. It concluded that the appropriate discount for lack of marketability was 25 percent, and the appropriate control premium was also 25 percent. "The application of the control premium and marketability discount is offsetting in this case." Thus, the court concluded that the fair market value of the stock redeemed by the corporation was $4.9 million, making the value of the gift made to decedent's son worth $1.9 million.

Estate of Magnin v. Commissioner (II)

The IRS' "more reliable" valuation accepted over estate valuation

Citation: T.C. Memo. 2001-31, 2001 Tax Ct. Memo LEXIS 41
Date of decision: February 12, 2001
Country: US
State or Federal: Federal
Court: United States Tax Court
Experts: Bryan Browning, ASA (for estate)
Stephen Stewart, ASA (for IRS)
Type of action: Estate and Gift Taxation
Judge: Ruwe
SIC: 5621 Women's Clothing Stores (except dress shops and bridal shops)

Key words: Control premium, Estate tax, Fair market value (FMV)

This case involves a hearing on remand from the Ninth Circuit to provide sufficient analysis of the consideration value of common and preferred stock in two closely held companies transferred and received by Cyril Magnin, the life estate holder. The issue appealed was whether, under Section 2036(a), Cyril received "adequate and full consideration" for the remainder interest he agreed to transfer to his children under the 1951 agreement he made with his father, Joseph Magnin.

Both experts valued the companies using the discounted cash flow and guideline public companies methods. However, their results varied greatly.

IRS valuation

Stephen Stewart of **KPMG Peat Marwick LLP,** the IRS' expert, valued the common stock by subtracting the preferred stock value from the companies' value as a whole. The preferred stock value was derived from comparing the actual dividend yield to the yield that would be demanded by an investor.

Stewart calculated the value of the consideration received and transferred by Cyril for both companies. He applied the following:

- Guideline public companies method with a 35% discount for lack of marketability, and

- Discounted cash flow method with 20% minority and 35% marketability discounts.

With a $158,000 value of Joseph's stock, Stewart valued the consideration Cyril received by factoring Cyril's age and voting control over the stock to arrive at a $30,500 valuation. He concluded that the remainder interest transferred by Cyril resulted in an overall value of $123,000.

Estate's valuation

Bryan Browning of **Valuation Research Corporation**, the estate's expert, similarly applied minority and marketability discounts after valuing the companies and subtracting the preferred stocks value. He valued the consideration by combining the shares owned by Joseph and Cyril, which constituted a controlling interest. This required a 40% control premium. Browning then valued Cyrils control value by deducting Josephs life estate value and Cyrils minority interest. The value of the remainder interest resulted from factoring the percentage of Cyrils ownership interest, the equity values of the companies, and his life interest. Browning valued the overall property transfer value at $42,000.

IRS valuation accepted as least erroneous and more reliable

The court criticized Brownings application of the willing buyer and willing seller standard. He assumed that the hypothetical buyer would be in the same position as Cyril where one could combine previously acquired shares to produce a control premium.

Browning also incorrectly applied a combined minority and marketability discount. The court noted that:

Discounts for marketability and minority interest are separate and distinct, and this fact must be taken into account when such discounts are applied in order to avoid distorting the valuation. While expert reports and the courts sometimes apply combined discount rates to determine the value of stock, this is a questionable procedure to use if specific rates are determined for each discount and then added together to reach the combined rate. See Pratt, et al., Valuing a Business: The Analysis and Appraisal of Closely Held Companies, 314 (3d ed. 1996). In order to ensure accuracy, the minority interest discount should be applied first and then the marketability and liquidity discount should be applied to this figure. Had this been done, the discounts would have yielded a combined discount rate of 51.25 percent.

Brownings testimony at trial produced further discrepancies regarding the reliability of his valuations. He discounted value from the guideline public companies method for minority interest, although he admitted that most appraisers view the market approach valuation as a minority interest value. According to his testimony, he discounted this valuation to produce a valuation that was more in line with the value he derived from the discounted cash flow method.

The court also noted that Stewart made a "troubling...large mistake" in his original valuation report, which he corrected after trial. He failed to subtract projected capital expenditures.

Although the court ruled that both experts erred in their calculations, the IRS valuation provided a better approximation of the values and was more reliable.

Northwest Investment Corp. v. Wallace

Case of First Impression: Does Statutory Fair Value Include a Control Premium?

Date of decision: July 13, 2007
State or Federal: State
State/Jurisdiction: Iowa
Court: Supreme Court
Type of action: Dissenting Shareholder
Experts: Wayne Brown and Ronald Nielsen (bank); Richard Maroney (minority shareholders)
Judge: Streit
SIC: 6022 State Commercial Banks (commercial banking)

As of now, seven states have adopted the 1999 amendments to the Model Business Corporation Act (MCBA)—specifically, its provisions disallowing consideration of minority and marketability discounts in fair value assessments (Connecticut, Idaho, Iowa, Maine, Mississippi, Virginia and West Virginia; Florida has adopted a variation). But none of these state courts had considered whether the new fair value definition mandates appraising the corporate shares on a marketable, control basis—until this Iowa case.

'It's all about control'

In 2003 a bank holding company effectively "squeezed out" three minority shareholders in a reverse stock split. Based on an expert fair value appraisal, the bank's directors paid the minority owners $33.23 per share for their respective interests and provided notice of their statutory appraisal rights.

The minority shareholders rejected the payment and, based on their expert appraisal, demanded $64 per share. The bank refused, and filed an appraisal action in Iowa district court. This time, it submitted a second appraisal, which posited a fair value of $48 per share. The bank paid the difference to the minority owners, plus interest. The minority shareholders turned this down and went to trial.

A case of 'dueling appraisals'

In its second appraisal, the bank's expert relied primarily on an income approach, capitalization of earnings method, giving it a 90% weight. He also used the guideline-company method, deriving an estimated price-to-book multiple from public comparables, applying it to the bank's adjusted book value and adding a 15% control premium (necessary because the public stock prices reflected minority interests). Weighting this approach 10%, he then "rolled up" the combined values through the holding company and its various interests and assets, concluding a fair value of the bank's shares at $48.

The expert for the minority shareholders used a combination of discounted cash flow (DCF) and market approach. For the latter, he considered guideline sales of publicly traded stock and sales of controlling interests in financial companies, creating for each a price-to-tangible book value ratio and a price-to-earnings multiple, for a total of four values. He added a 40% control premium to the DCF value and the two valuations based on publicly traded stock transactions. (Sales of controlling interest in financial institutions already accounted for the premium.) Averaging the five values, which ranged from approximately $61 per share to $73, he determined the fair value of the bank's stock at $64 per share.

Prior inconsistent valuations

One serious evidentiary problem with the bank's appraisal: It was "significantly lower" than recent appraisals done for the bank's employee stock option plan and its own reverse stock split. The district court found these multiple inconsistent appraisals of substantially the same assets "difficult if not impossible to reconcile." Second, the court also could find no rational basis for the different weights accorded the valuation methods, and it simply disagreed with the bank's position that a "well-run, high-performing business....should either have no or very little control premium added to determine fair value."

The district court adopted the "more credible" fair value appraisal by the minority shareholders' expert, including his addition of a control premium. On appeal, in reviewing the applicability of a control premium, the Iowa Supreme Court looked to the official drafters' comments to the 1999 MCBA amendments; in particular, their explanation for precluding minority and marketability discounts from a fair value appraisal. Their intent:

> ...to adopt a more modern view that appraisal should generally award a shareholder his or her *proportional interest in the corporation after valuing the corporation as a whole,* rather than the value of the shareholder's shares when valued alone (Court's emphasis).

"If an appraiser is valuing the corporation as a whole," the Court added, "then a control premium is certainly proper" (citing *Valuing a Business: The Analysis and Appraisal of Closely Held Companies*, 4th ed., by "leading authority" Shannon Pratt). Further, by disallowing discounts for lack of marketability and control, the legislature "implicitly required shares to be valued on a marketable, control interest basis." A control premium, if supported by the evidence, is therefore appropriate.

A note on synergy

Lastly, the bank argued that the control premium was "inflated with synergistic value because the market data, upon which [it] is based, included corporate mergers." The bank's fair value should be determined on a standalone basis rather than in a possible merger.

The minority shareholders did not present evidence that a merger was in the bank's future or that its value should be based on anything but a going concern, standalone basis. "Nevertheless, there is nothing wrong with [the dissenters' expert] basing his opinion, in part, on the aggregations of actual sales data involving mergers and acquisitions," as this evidence reflected the market place. While the expert conceded that synergistic value was likely embedded in the data, comparable sales transactions are still "the best empirical evidence generally available to quantify a control premium," the Court said, once again citing Pratt for proposition—and the reminder that analysts should be simply be aware of synergies included in the underlying data and adjust accordingly.

Based on the available data, the minority shareholders' expert determined control premiums ranging from 36% to 52% for companies comparable to the bank. His "conservative approach" also attempted to remove any marketplace distortions. "Although we cannot be certain what effect, if any, synergistic value had on [the expert's] calculations," the Court concluded, "it is more appropriate to accept [his] control premium in order to eliminate the [prohibited] minority discount ... than to make no adjustment at all."

Estate of Simplot v. Commissioner (II)

Simplot reversed by Ninth Circuit; control premium for voting shares incorrectly applied

Citation: 249 F.3d 1191, 2001 U.S. App. LEXIS 9220
Date of decision: May 14, 2001
Country: US
State or Federal: Federal
State/Jurisdiction: 9th Circuit
Court: United States Court of Appeals
Experts: J. Paul Much (for estate), John R. Ettelson (for estate), Herbert Spiro (for IRS), Gilbert Matthews (for IRS)
Type of action: Estate and Gift Taxation
Judge: Noonan
SIC: 0191 General Farms, Primarily Crop

Key words: Control premium, Estate tax, Fair market value (FMV), Minority interest

This case is the Ninth Circuit Court of Appeals' decision on appeal of *Estate of Simplot v. Commissioner,* 112 T.C. No.13 (1999),1 which was abstracted in the May 1999 issue of *Shannon Pratt's Business Valuation Update.* The U.S. Tax Court had ruled in favor of the IRS, rejecting the estate's valuation expert and assigning a 3% premium to the block of Class A voting stock in **J.R. Simplot Co.** (Simplot). The Ninth Circuit reversed the Tax Court's ruling and ordered entry of judgment in favor of the estate on remand because "the Tax Court erroneously attributed a premium to minority voting stock in the J.R. Simplot Co."

Background on Simplot

Richard R. Simplot (decedent) died on June 24, 1993. His estate held a 23.55% minority interest of the voting class and a 2.79% minority interest of the nonvoting class of the common stock of Simplot. Simplot had reported sales of $1.8 billion, net income of $37.8 million for the fiscal year ending Aug. 31, 1993, and was one of the two largest potato processors in the world.

The company also owned 5.3 million shares and 13% of the common stock of Micron Technology, Inc., a publicly traded manufacturer of semiconductor memory components and personal computers. At the date of death, the market value of the Micron stock was $182.1 million with trapped-in capital gains of $169 million.

At the date of valuation there were 76.445 voting shares (Class A) and 141,288.584 nonvoting shares (Class B) reflecting one share of voting stock per 1,848 shares of nonvoting stock. The voting shares were owned by decedent and his siblings as shown in Table 1 above, right.

The majority of the nonvoting shares-62.83%-were owned by a trust for the descendants of decedent, Don, Gay, and Scott. The Class A and B shares had equal rights to dividends and to liquidation distributions even though Simplot never paid out dividends. A right of first refusal applied to anyone who wished to sell Class A shares. Any shareholder had to wait 360 days before selling voting shares to an outsider.

The Tax Court decision

In *Estate of Simplot v. Commissioner,* 112 T.C. No.13 (1999), the Tax Court reviewed a valuation of the Simplot stock by the Commissioner of Internal Revenue that resulted in a $801,994 value per share of Class A stock and $3,585 per share of Class B stock. The experts were **Herbert Spiro** and **Gilbert Matthews** for the IRS and **J. Paul Much** and **John R. Ettelson** for the Estate of Richard R. Simplot (Estate).

Table 1		
Stockholder	Number of shares	Percent of total shares
Decedent	18	23.55
Don Simplot	18	23.55
Gay Simplot Otter	18	23.55
Scott Simplot	22.445	29.35
Total	76.445	100

There were four issues before the court:

1. The marketable minority interest value of Simplot.
2. Treatment of the trapped-in-capital gains pertaining to Micron stock.
3. The appropriate discount for lack of marketability for both classes of shares.
4. Whether a premium should be applied to the Estate's Class A voting shares.

The Tax Court used inputs from both sides' experts and decided without much discussion on the first three issues as follows:

1. The fair market value of the Simplot stock on a marketable minority interest basis was $830 million, of which $720 represented operating value and $110 non-operating value of Micron stock.
2. The court accepted the advice of both appraisers that the full amount of the trapped-in-capital gains tax liability should be deducted from the Simplot value.
3. The issue of the discount for lack of marketability was decided almost without comment at a 35% marketability discount for the Class A voting shares and 40% marketability discount for the Class B nonvoting shares.

The premium for the voting shares

Regarding the premium for the Class A voting shares, the IRS's experts placed a premium on the voting stock because of the unbalanced ratio of voting to nonvoting shares. The Estates experts offered empirical evidence that the differential between the two classes should be minimal and that the minority interest in the Class A stock could not provide increased economic benefit to the shareholders.

The court adopted the position of the IRSs experts and assigned a 3% premium to the block of Class A voting shares in Simplot. The premium was based on the whole equity value of the company of $830 million for a total of $ 24.9 million. This decision was based on the Tax Courts observation that a hypothetical buyer of the 18 voting shares "would gain access to the 'inner circle of J.R. Simplot Co. and by having a seat at the Class A shareholders table, over time, the hypothetical buyer potentially could position itself to play a role in the Company."

The court also considered some of the characteristics of the hypothetical buyer as being "well financed, with a long-term investment horizon and no expectations of near-term benefits." The court also noted that in the future the buyer of the 18 shares could become the controlling owner because of the shares being divided among many Simplot descendants.

Considering all the valuation elements, the Tax Court calculated the value of the Simplot Class A voting shares as shown in Table 2 below.

Ninth Circuit finds three major errors in Tax Courts ruling

The Ninth Circuit noted at the beginning of its analysis that the estate tax is based on the "value of the property in the decedents hands at the time of its transfer by death." The Ninth Circuit determined that the Tax Court committed errors in the following three areas:

- Hypothetical buyer standard
- Calculation of the voting stock premium for the Estate shares
- Insufficient evidence for a control premium

Hypothetical buyer standard

The Ninth Circuit noted that the Tax Court departed from the willing buyer/seller standard by believing that "the hypothetical sale should not be considered in a vacuum isolated from the actual facts that affect value." The Ninth Circuit also found that the Tax Court violated the law by constructing particular possible purchasers. The appeals court further considered that the facts presented as factors influencing the premium calculations were merely speculations and imaginary scenarios as to the purchasers characteristics.

Table 2

Marketable minority value of Simplot	$830 million
Class A and Class B shares (76.445 + 141,296.4)	141,372.85
Marketable minority value of Simplot per share ($830 million/141,372.85)	$5,871.32
Voting stock premium per share ($830 million*3%)/76.445	$325,724.38
Class A value per share before discount	$331,595.70
Discount for lack of marketability $331,595.38*35%	$116,058.50
Class A value per share	$215,539

Calculation of voting shares premium

The Tax Court also erred in calculating the control premium pertaining to all the Class A voting shares and then dividing it equally among them. There was no reason to believe that the value attributable to the control of Simplot could be proportionally attributed to a fraction of the total shares. The Ninth Circuit Court noted that "the Tax Court valued an asset not before it - all the Class A stock representing control."

Insufficient evidence for control premium

The Ninth Circuit finally noted that even a controlling block of stock is to be valued at a premium for estate tax purposes only if the Commissioner can show that the buyer will enjoy an increased economic advantage from control. In the Ninth Circuits opinion, the 18-share minority interest in the Class A voting stock did not offer a clear increased advantage to the shareholders, except for the speculative factors presented by the Tax Court.

The Ninth Circuit finally noted: "In Richard Simplots hands at the time of transfer his stock was worth what a willing buyer would have paid for the economic benefits presently attached to the stock. By this standard, a minority holding Class A share was worth no more than a Class B share."

The judgment of the Tax Court was accordingly reversed and the case remanded for entry of judgment in favor of the Estate.

Judge Fletcher dissents

Circuit Judge W. Fletcher dissented from this opinion, believing the Tax Court was correct in its decision and valuation of the Class A voting shares.

Judge Fletcher based his dissent on the assumption that any of the Simplot surviving Class A shareholders would probably pay a high premium in order to achieve control. In his opinion, any willing buyer and seller negotiating a price for the 18 shares would be aware of this potential premium. Judge Fletcher finalized his dissent with an "appeal to economic reality."

Under the majoritys view, there is no fair market value whatsoever for the right to vote the 18 A shares. In its view, one A share is worth precisely the same as one B share. The majority therefore concludes that the fair market value of shares representing 23.5% of the voting shares of a company with sales of $1.8 billion and an equity value of $830 million is only $54,450.

AN Comment: **Since Mr. Chris Mercer abstracted and analyzed the initial decision of the Tax Court in the May 1999 issue of the BVU, we have again asked for his**

insights in the Ninth Circuits reversal of the case. We have also asked for Gilbert Matthews opinion on the Ninth Circuits decision and he gladly accepted to share his comments on how this decision is affecting the taxpayers and the appraisal community in the July issue of the BVU.

Chris Mercers* Comment: My initial review of Simplot was very pointedly critical on the issue of the voting/nonvoting premium advanced by Spiro and Matthews, experts for the IRS, and adopted by the Tax Court. My conclusion was that they had reached some kind of value, but that it was not fair market value as I have come to understand the concept. The Ninth Circuit agreed with my position, referring to the method as "speculation." Some additional perspective on the nature of this "speculation" is in order.

Readers should not lose sight of the fact that the subject investments were a 23.55% minority interest of the voting class of Simplot (the Company) and a 2.79% minority interest of the nonvoting class. With only one share of voting stock per 1,848 nonvoting shares, the equity capital structure was unusual. But the capital structure of a company is not an economic driver of value, per se.

To illustrate, see accompanying Table 3, p. 8, which replicates the Tax Courts decision using a 3.0% enterprise value "Simplot Premium" for the voting class. Varying nothing but the nonvoting/voting ratio from 1,848/1 to 1/1, the freely traded values range from $331,359 per share to $6,047 per share for the voting shares, and the percentage voting premium varies from 5,719% to 6%.

Now, refer to Table 4, p. 8, which lowers the "Simplot Premium" to 1.0%, and per share values and percentage voting premiums vary markedly for each indicated equity structure and across structures.

The Simplot *analysis would suggest that the two most important determinants of the value of voting shares, after freely traded value is established, are the nonvoting/voting mix of the capital structure and the "Simplot Premium." Business appraisers have no control or influence over the former, and know little or nothing about the latter.*

The Tax Courts opinion in Simplot *created a great deal of concern for business appraisers and for estate planning attorneys. Too many appraisers believe that they should rely upon cases like* Simplot *as providing valuation precedent for use in appraisals. Unfortunately, this should not be the case. I have long argued that it is the job of business appraisers to advance economic arguments on valuation questions to the courts, and it is the job of the courts to decide, based on those economic arguments.*

For many years, business appraisers considered that it was inappropriate to tax-affect imbedded capital gains in C corporation asset holding entities because of a long series of cases in which the Tax Court refused to recognize this imbedded liability. Yet, finally, in Davis, Eisenberg, *and* Simplot, *it is now accepted that this liability is really an economic issue that must be considered.*

In Simplot, *the taxpayers experts stuck to their guns and lost on the issue of the voting versus nonvoting premium in Tax Court. However, the taxpayers believed in their arguments sufficiently to take the unusual step of appealing the Tax Courts decision. In the appellate forum, the Tax Courts conclusions (and the arguments of Spiro and Matthews) were found guilty of exercising in "speculation."*

Why? Fair market value is grounded in economic reality. Spiro, Matthews, and the Tax Court failed to consider how the hypothetical (or, in their cases, particular) purchaser would achieve a rate of return on his or her investment in Class A voting shares. And they failed to consider the risk of almost total loss of investment if the company were sold or merged with another, in which case the Class A voting shares and the Class B nonvoting shares would be treated equally. In doing so, they failed to consider the economic realities of the required hypothetical investment in Class A voting shares, and reached conclusions that represented something other than fair market value, which was the required standard of value for estate tax purposes. I will let the attorneys in your readership deal with the dissenting opinion. And I wont address the Ninth Circuits conclusion of no differential between the voting and nonvoting shares, when a small differential might have been justified based on market evidence.

Slattery v. U.S.

Lost Value of Failed Bank Turns on Expert Evidence of Market Cap and Control

Citation: 2009 WL 3082360 (C. A. Fed.)
Date of decision: Sept. 29, 2009
Country: US
State or Federal: Federal
State/Jurisdiction: Federal Circuit
Court: United States Court of Appeals
Type of action: Contract
Experts: Dr. John Flattery (plaintiff bank); Dr. Goldstein (government/defendant)
Judge: Newman

This is likely among the last of the litigation to emerge from the savings and loan scandals of the late 1970s and early 1980s—a turbulent financial time exacerbated by an economic recession and high interest rates (sound familiar?). These cases may very well set the precedent for those arising from the current financial turmoil, in particular as they establish evidentiary standards for economic damages relating to financial institutions and other troubled asset values.

Federal intervention leads to bank failure. To ameliorate the extreme economic pressure on banks during the S&L crisis, the Federal Deposit Insurance Corporation (FDIC) encouraged "healthy" institutions to merge with failing entities, thus avoiding a call on federal funds. Accordingly, in April 1982, the FDIC sought to merge Western Savings Fund with the more solid Meritor Savings Bank by providing $294 million in financial incentives plus the following accounting expedient, as provided in a written memorandum of understanding (MOU):

The difference between the liabilities assumed and the total of the market value of the Western assets, less reserves, may be treated as goodwill and amortized on a straight line basis up to fifteen (15) years...

Permitting goodwill to be measured as a form of capital (excess of the acquired bank's liabilities over the value of its asset) effectively treated the liabilities as capital assets for regulatory compliance purposes and allowed the merged entity to meet the then-current 5% capital requirement for savings banks. With the 1982 MOU, Meritor completed the merger and rescued Western from certain liquidation.

As the nation's economic troubles persisted, however, the FDIC raised capital minimums to 5.5%. In a 1988 MOU, it required Meritor to meet a higher 6.5% standard or submit to a $200 million restructuring plan to "improve its financial health." Meritor complied, largely by selling off valuable branches. By 1991, however, Meritor still made the government's list of "projected bank failures" and in a 1992 MOU, the FDIC raised the bank's capital requirements to 8.5% (primary) and 10.5% (risk-based), although it still permitted the inclusion of goodwill. Not long after, the FDIC issued a regulation requiring insured banks to establish a minimum ratio of tangible capital to total assets of 2%. Meritor sold additional assets but couldn't lift its tangible ratio above 0.66%, despite maintaining a total capital ratio of 7.5%, including goodwill.

The FDIC revoked the bank's insured status in December 1992 for failing to comply with the new regulations and Meritor's assets were seized.

Shareholders sue for $696 million. On behalf of all the bank's shareholders, Meritor's owner brought a derivative action against the FDIC for breach of contract, and after a five-month trial the Court of Federal Claims found the government liable. The FDIC first breached the 1982 MOU when it "effectively ignored Meritor's right to rely on goodwill as capital...and required it to enter into the 1988 MOU, which raised its total capital requirements." Moreover, by forcing the bank to sell valuable branches, the 1988 MOU led directly to "the downward death spiral for Meritor," the Court of Claims said. Within fewer than five years, the bank's assets shrank from $19 billion to $5.9 billion and it was "doomed."

The court held additional proceedings to determine damages. After hearing expert testimony from both sides it awarded Meritor just over $373 million based on a theory of lost business value. The government appealed both aspects of the verdict and the shareholders appealed only the damages, claiming the award should have reflected its alternative theory based on avoided liquidation costs of $696 million.

In the first portion of a lengthy opinion, the U.S. Court of Appeals affirmed the lower court's liability rulings. Turning to damages next, the court first discussed Meritor's theory of lost business value. In particular, Meritor's expert Dr.

John Finnerty (Finnerty Economic Consulting LLC and Fordham Univ., New York City) calculated the bank's actual stock market valuation in August 1988—just before the government's first breach—at $171 million. He calculated an additional market value, correcting for the negative publicity surrounding the FDIC's actions against the bank, of $196 million. After applying a 50% control premium to each figure, he averaged the two and arrived at $276 million, or the amount adopted by the trial court as "expectancy damages." (The court also added $67 million in "non-overlapping restitution" for a total of $373 million.)

The government did not dispute the basic theory of lost business value; instead, it claimed that the trial court used the incorrect valuation date (1988). Preferable was the date of the bank's seizure in 1992 because shareholders continued to control operations until then. According to the government's expert, "even without the FDIC's breach Meritor would have had to shrink during the period from 1987-1992 by at least $10 billion in assets...to satisfy the prevailing 5.5% capital requirements with hypothetical losses of $650.9 million." These losses should be set off against the bank's actual market value in 1988, the expert maintained, thereby reducing damages to zero.

The Court of Appeals found this argument unpersuasive (as had the trial court). The series of events that led to the bank's "death spiral" would not have occurred at all "but for" the government's 1988 breach and the FDIC's ensuing actions, including its "distaste for goodwill." Although the government's expert predicted losses, he also predicted a full return to profitability, "a goal that was never realized because of the FDIC's breaches that led to seizure of the bank," the court explained. Absent the breaches, the court held that it was unlikely that Meritor would have failed during the relevant time period, and the government's theory failed to rebut this finding.

Contesting the control premium. The bank defended the trial court's acceptance of a 50% control premium in adopting the $276 million damages award. Although Meritor's expert testified that he would not normally add a premium to the bank's stock market capitalization, he did say that acquirers of a majority interest would pay a premium for controlling the entire corporation. By contrast, the government argued that a control premium applied *only* to an acquisition context and did not reflect an "inherent aspect of the bank's market value." When assessing a lost business, shareholder value based on control was "irrelevant," its expert said.

Both sides cited precedent in support of their positions, but neither side was "sufficiently on point," the appellate court ruled. "The trial court's application of a control premium to determine Meritor's fair market value was a fact determination based on extensive and detailed expert testimony," and it deemed the bank's expert more persuasive, including his testimony that "even an underperforming bank, if it has strong franchise value based on depositor loyalty...commands a high control premium." Finding no clear error in the lower court determination, the appellate court held that in this case, a lost business could be measured by the entire franchise value, including a control premium.

The court did find error in the award of "restitution damages," however. The trial court gave the bank both the net cost of entering the contract with the government and the value lost due to its breach. And "while the two sums are measured by different transactions that do not technically 'overlap,' they are incompatible as measures of damages for breach," the court held, and it reversed the additional $67 million.

As a final point, the bank argued its alternative liquidation theory of damages ($696 million). This represented restitution as measured by the financial benefits realized when the FDIC induced Meritor's merger with Western Bank. The trial court largely agreed with the factual predicate: If the bank hadn't agreed to the merger, then the FDIC would have paid $696 million to liquidate Western. After accounting for the $294 million paid to Meritor to complete the merger, the FDIC realized a total cost savings of $402 million.

Despite finding a legal basis for awarding this amount in general contract cases, the trial court cited inadequate support in *Winstar* cases (those following the U.S. Supreme Court's leading decision in *Winstar, Inc. v. U.S.*, 518 U.S. 839 (1996), which established government liability for recognizing supervisory goodwill and then passing legislation to restrict or prohibit it). "The Federal circuit has...affirmed restitution of only direct monetary payments...as part of contractual performance," the trial court explained, in reference to its denying the restitution theory of damages, and the U.S. Court of Appeals affirmed.

In re Toys "R" Us, Inc., Shareholder Litigation

Control premium not needed for DCF analysis using Gordon growth model

Citation: 2005 Del. Ch. LEXIS 90
Date of decision: June 22, 2005
Country: US
State or Federal: State
State/Jurisdiction: Delaware
Court: Court of Chancery
Type of action: Breach of Fiduciary Duty
Judge: Strine
SIC: 5945 Hobby, Toy, and Game Stores

Key words: Shareholder action, Control premium, Discounted cash flow method (DCF), Comparable transactions method, Gordon Growth Capitalization Model

The board of **Toys "R" Us, Inc.** (the Company) decided to sell the corporation to **Kohlberg Kravis Roberts & Co.** ("the KKR Group") for $26.75 per share. The company's shareholders claimed that the directors failed to maximize shareholder value in the deal. One of the issues was whether the board's financial advisor, **Credit Suisse First Boston** (First Boston), correctly excluded a control premium in its assessment of the company's value, and, thus, whether the board failed to reasonably consider the value of all relevant alternatives.

Valuation facts

The Company had three divisions: Global Toys, Babies "R" Us (Babies), and Toys Japan. Babies had been subsidized by Global Toys, whereby overhead that Babies used was actually charged to the Global Toys division, a practice that resulted in an inflation of the Babies division's profits to the corresponding detriment of the profits of Global Toys. The board's original plan was to sell only Global Toys, but eventually, the KKR Group made a bid for the entire Company.

First Boston presented a "sum of the parts" valuation of the Company. The resulting value range for the entire company was between $4.325 billion and $6.125 billion (or between $14.11 and $22.19 per share). Of those values, Global Toys was valued at between $2.85 billion and $3.75 billion (or between $11.40 and $15.00 per share). By comparison, Babies was valued at between $1.7 billion and $2.1 billion (or between $6.80 and $8.40 per share).

When valuing Babies, First Boston used a discounted cash flow (DCF) valuation, the base of which valued Babies at between $1.8 to $2.375 billion, or $7.96 to $10.51 per share. The second was a comparable transactions analysis that valued Babies between $1.75 to $2.25 billion, or $7.74 to $9.96 per share. However, First Boston explicitly indicated that its valuation of Babies did not include a control premium.

The plaintiff shareholders argued that, therefore, the board was not informed that Babies was worth more than First Boston had led the board to believe it was worth, given that a control premium should have been added to First Boston's value range, and that the Company was worth well above KKR Group's $26.75 bid.

Holding and rationale

The Delaware Chancery Court rejected this argument for several reasons, the most important of which was that it was not unreasonable for First Boston to focus on valuing Babies as if it was not going to be sold, because, initially, the plan was to not sell that division. Once Global Toys was sold, the Company's stockholders would own shares in a corporation that was functionally Babies. Those shares would trade on a minority basis in the marketplace. Under that scenario, Company stockholders would not have access to a control premium on Babies until it was sold, in an indefinite time frame sometime in the future.

The court also noted that a DCF conducted using the Gordon growth model, as First Boston's updated DCF did, does not embed a minority discount. Rather, that value is a value of the entity itself. The court concluded that adding a control premium on top of a DCF is not intuitively or theoretically logical. Indeed, the court reasoned that because a DCF model using the Gordon growth model is not infected by a minority discount, it is the model most consistent with what the Company's stockholders would receive in an appraisal—their pro rata share of the Company's value.

For these reasons, the court ruled that the board had before it precisely the kind of valuation information it was supposed to have under Delaware law.

BVR
What It's Worth
www.BVResources.com

Bulletproof your valuation conclusions with BVR's comprehensive line of product offerings.

Every top firm depends on BVR for authoritative market data, continuing professional education, and expert opinion. So, turn to BVR whenever you need unimpeachable business valuation conclusions for any purpose. BVR's market databases, publications, and analysis have won in the courtroom—and the boardroom—for over a dozen years. All BVR products include a subscription to the profession's leading weekly eNewsletter, BVWire™, absolutely FREE!

Our expansive line of products include:

- Pratt's Stats®
- Public Stats™
- BIZCOMPS®
- Mergerstat®/BVR Control Premium Study™
- The FMV Restricted Stock Study™
- Valuation Advisors' Discount for Lack of Marketability Study™
- Integra 5-Year Industry Data Reports
- **NEW!** Duff & Phelps Risk Premium Reports
- Business Valuation Update™
- Deluxe BVUpdate™
- Annual Guides and Books
- Business Reference Guide Online Database
- Economic Outlook Update™
- BVLaw™
- BVResearch™
- Special reports, guides, and books
- Continuing Professional Education (CPE)
- BVNewsletter™ service
- BVBasics™ Seminar Package
- Teleconferences and Webinars
- Live Conferences
- BV Firm Marketing Services
- Butler Pinkerton Model™ - Total Cost of Equity (TCOE) and Public company Specific Risk Calculator

Learn more at www.BVResources.com

Business Valuation Resources, LLC . 1000 SW Broadway, Suite 1200 . Portland OR 97205
Phone: (503) 291-7963 . Fax: (503) 291-7955 . Email: CustomerService@BVResources.com

www.ingramcontent.com/pod-product-compliance
Lightning Source LLC
LaVergne TN
LVHW082352200926
848481LV00012B/3540